A NEO-CLASSICAL THEORY
OF ECONOMIC GROWTH

Books by J. E. Meade
GEOMETRY OF INTERNATIONAL TRADE
PLANNING AND THE PRICE MECHANISM
PROBLEMS OF ECONOMIC UNION
(*Allen & Unwin*)

INTRODUCTION TO ECONOMIC ANALYSIS AND POLICY
THEORY OF INTERNATIONAL ECONOMIC POLICY
(*Oxford University Press*)

THE THEORY OF CUSTOMS UNIONS
(*North-Holland Publishing Company*)

THE CONTROL OF INFLATION
(*Cambridge University Press*)

A Neo-Classical Theory
of Economic Growth

BY

J. E. MEADE

C.B., F.B.A.

REVISED NEW EDITION

Ruskin House
GEORGE ALLEN & UNWIN LTD
MUSEUM STREET LONDON

First Published in 1961

Revised Second Edition 1962

*Printed in Great Britain
in* 11 *on* 12 *point Plantin type
by J. W. Arrowsmith Ltd
Bristol*

PREFACE TO THE FIRST EDITION

There is already an extensive literature on the theory of economic growth and the publication of yet one more work on the subject needs some explanation. This book falls essentially into two parts, (i) the main text, and (ii) the long Appendix II; and these two parts serve rather different purposes and demand, therefore, rather different justifications.

The main text makes little, if any, claim to originality. It is merely a systematic exposition of how a straightforward classical economic system would behave as it grew through time as a result of population growth, capital accumulation, and technical progress. These chapters are written in such a way that they should be intelligible to any serious student of economic theory; they demand no elaborate mathematical techniques.

I have thought it worthwhile to publish these chapters because most of the systematic works which have been published recently on the theory of economic growth depart essentially in one way or another from these classical assumptions. And this is apt to have an unfortunate effect upon the mind of the student, who is thereby tempted—if not positively compelled—to use the classical set of tools when he is considering problems in comparative statics (for example, problems concerned with the allocation of resources as between different uses) and a quite different set of tools when he is considering rates of growth in the economy.

Yet such a dichotomy can at least in part be avoided. There is no essential difficulty in setting a classical system to grow. A number of distinguished economists—I mention the names of Solow, Samuelson, Little, Hicks, and Swan—have made important contributions in showing how a classical system would grow. These contributions are important separate pieces of a general picture; and it is simply this general picture which I have tried to draw. Of course, in fact economic growth has much to do with conditions which I have scarcely discussed—economies of large-scale production, external economies, market forms other than the perfectly competitive, and so on. Such a picture as I have drawn needs modification and expansion in many ways to make it relevant to many of the problems of growth in the real world. But I greatly hope that it may serve for the serious student of economic theory as a useful bridge between classical economic analysis and modern theories of economic growth.

As soon as one tries to outline the way in which a classical economic system would behave in the process of economic growth, one comes up against a central problem, namely what would happen to, and what would be the effect of changes in, the prices of one product in terms of another and, in particular, the price of capital goods in terms of consumption goods. This issue I have tried to explore systematically and with the aid of some mathematics in my long Appendix II. I hope that in that Appendix I may have advanced a little our understanding of this central problem.

It is impossible to enumerate all the persons who, in addition to those I have already mentioned, have by ideas expressed in writing or conversation influenced my way of thinking on this subject. But as is the case with all writers on this subject, I owe much to the pioneer work of Harrod and Domar, as will, I think, be obvious from a reading of this book.

I owe another very special debt of gratitude to my immediate colleagues. It is impossible to study economics in present-day Cambridge without being affected by the ferment of ideas on this subject; and the fact that I have come to work in Cambridge is the immediate cause of this attempt to present a bridge between classical theory and the modern interest in the theory of economic growth. This ferment of ideas centres round the well-known work of Mrs Robinson, Mr Kaldor, Mr Champernowne, Professor Kahn, and Dr Sen. To these I am indeed in debt; for they have all read and commented on part or the whole of my work at one stage or another. Mrs Robinson in particular has been an indefatigable, severe, but friendly critic of what I have done. It is so clear that they will not like my classical system, that it is hardly necessary for me to add the conventional remark that they must not be held responsible for any errors which I have committed. My thanks are due also to Professor Stone for reading my manuscript. He has himself been independently constructing a system very similar to mine; and it is reassuring to know that we confirm each other's results.

Finally, I would like to thank my colleague Mr Roy for performing for me the integrations on pages 161 and 166 of my Appendix II, which—as the reader will realise—constitute the basic steps towards the conclusions of that Appendix.

J. E. MEADE

Christ's College
  Cambridge
December, 1959

PREFACE TO THE SECOND EDITION

In revising this book for a second edition I have taken the opportunity of making some corrections. In particular I have recast much of Chapter 3 to take account of an important criticism made by Professor Sir Dennis Robertson to whom I am also indebted for a number of minor corrections. Section (2) of Appendix I has been added to establish a firm basis for what is now said in Chapter 3.

It has become clear to me that there are many useful ways in which the analysis used in the first edition of this book can readily be extended, and I have taken this opportunity to include some of them.

(1) In Chapter 4 (pages 39 to 42) and in the new Section (3) of Appendix I I have said something of the path along which an economy would move into a state of steady growth.

(2) In Chapter 4 (pages 42 to 45) and in the new Section (4) of Appendix I I have analysed the paradoxical fact that the proportion of income saved affects the stock of capital, but not the rate of capital accumulation, in a state of steady economic growth.

(3) In Chapter 4 (pages 45 and 46) I have dealt more adequately with the effect of population growth upon the standard of living—a consideration which is of the utmost importance in the real world for many economies.

(4) In the new Chapter 5 and in the new Section (5) of Appendix I I have shown how the 'neo-classical' analysis can be used not only to consider growth in conditions of full employment (as was done in the first edition of this book) but also to consider growth in conditions of overpopulation in which there is an indefinitely large reserve of unemployed labour available at the current real wage rate.

But the basic assumptions and analysis of the book remain unchanged. It still does not deal (i) with the dynamic processes of movements off the path of equilibrium growth, (ii) with the effects of monopolistic forms of production and marketing, (iii) with the existence of a large diversity of different products, both capital goods and consumption goods, and (iv) with the rigidity in the forms of real capital over the life-span of particular instruments of production and with the consequent importance of uncertainty and errors of forecasting in determining the path of economic growth.

The reader must decide for himself how much light the present book, in spite of these deficiencies, throws on the problems of the real world. I myself am not dazzled by it, but I would nevertheless claim that it can help to illuminate some otherwise obscure relationships. I would comment in the following way on the four deficiencies enumerated above.

(i) This book is certainly not classical in the sense of being pre-Keynesian. It is, however, based on the assumption of an ideally successful Keynesian policy which at every point of time manages to keep the value of investment at the desired level. It is not difficult in principle to graft on to this certain time lags between (a) any change in market conditions and the subsequent action of the authorities in adopting inflationary or deflationary policies, (b) any change in monetary policy and the consequent effect on entrepreneurs' expenditure on investment, and (c) any change in individuals' incomes and the consequential change in their expenditures on consumption. The effect of this would be to determine the dynamic movements of the growing system off the path of equilibrium growth. In a forthcoming article Professor A. W. H. Phillips has already done just this in large measure—indeed completely for a special case of the production function used in this book.

(ii) This book is classical in the sense that it is built on the assumption of perfect competition and of payments to factors equal to the value of their marginal products. I do not, of course, regard this as an accurate description of much that goes on in many markets in the real world. But it is the simplest special case of a relationship of great importance in the real world. What ever may be the market forms, an entrepreneur in deciding whether to take on more of any agent, or group of agents, of production will be influenced by the relationship between the cost to him of that agent or group of agents and the value to him of the change in his output. If this is so, two consequences follow. First, the forms of techniques of production used (i.e. the ratios between the various agents of production) will be influenced by the relative prices of these agents of production. Second, the distribution of income will be greatly influenced by the existing production and marketing possibilities taken in conjunction with the available supplies of the various agents of production, as entrepreneurs bid heavily against each other in their attempts to take on more of the agents whose cost is exceptionally low compared with the value of what they could add to output. This means that a theory of equilibrium growth cannot be based upon Mr Kaldor's theory of distribution. Suppose that in conditions of full employment entrepreneurs decide to spend more on capital development. This might conceivably cause, through the multiplier, an inflation of demand, a rise in prices, a shift of real income from unchanged money wages to greatly increased money profits, and thus, because more is saved out of profits than out of wages, a rise in savings equal to the initial rise in investment. But can it really be maintained that if wage rates remained unchanged but prices and selling prospects for all products greatly improved, entrepreneurs would not bid up the wage rate against each other? How else can one explain the notorious phenomenon of wage drift? Would not the authorities at some point have to take action to correct or offset the initial inflation of investment? Mr Kaldor's theory of distribution is more appropriate for the explanation of short-run inflation than of long-run growth. My assumption of perfect competition in the theory of equilibrium growth should, if possible, be appropriately modified; but it is a better starting point than a complete divorce between factor prices, product prices, and the competition of employers for factors of production.

(iii) It would be very desirable to allow for the existence of many different consumption goods and capital goods. I confess that I have not yet acquired the mathematical techniques necessary to deal with this. But I have a strong hunch that the main result would be not very substantially to alter the basic conclusions of the present analysis, but very greatly to increase the possibility of substitution between the various factors of production. For a fall in the cost of using certain machines relatively to the cost of employing labour would now not only give an incentive to entrepreneurs to use a higher ratio of these machines to labour in every line of production; but it would also give an incentive to consumers to buy more of the cheaper machine-intensive, and less of the more expensive labour-intensive, products and a incentive to entrepreneurs to use as instruments of production capital goods which were themselves machine-intensive rather than labour-intensive in their production. A main purpose of using a neo-classical analysis for the theory of growth is to allow for substitutability between factors; and this purpose is reinforced in a world of many products.

(iv) The assumptions made in this book of perfect malleability of machines and of depreciation by evaporation (see pages 6 and 7) do lead to a gross neglect of errors of foresight and problems of uncertainty. These certainly should be one of the main features of a complete theory of economic growth. In my opinion this is much the most serious criticism of the type of analysis used in this book. It would certainly be desirable to repair this omission. I can only promise to continue to think about these matters and to try to do better in the future.

There remains one other way in which this book is distinctly 'classical' in spirit. The analysis is based upon the existence of the three classical factors of production—land, labour, and capital. In fact in the real world factors of production do fall into the three broad categories of natural resources, human effort, and man-made instruments. The interrelationships between these three categories is of great importance in economic growth; and in this second edition I have paid even more attention to them than was done in the original version of this book.

J. E. MEADE

Christ's College
  Cambridge
  July, 1961

CONTENTS

		page
PREFACE TO THE FIRST EDITION		v
PREFACE TO THE SECOND EDITION		viii

1. *Introduction* — 1
2. *Three Determinants of the Rate of Economic Growth* — 8
3. *Changes in the Rate of Economic Growth* — 19
4. *The State of Steady Economic Growth* — 30
5. *The Overpopulated Economy* — 47
6. *An Alternative Treatment of Technical Progress* — 55
7. *The Rigidity of Machinery* — 61
8. *The Price of Capital Goods* — 71
9. *Depreciation and Replacement* — 79

APPENDIX I. *One Product and Three Factors* — 93
    (1) The Elasticities of Substitution between Three Factors
    (2) Changes in the Rate of Economic Growth
    (3) The Approach to the State of Steady Growth
    (4) The Level of Savings in the State of Steady Growth
    (5) The Case of Overpopulation

APPENDIX II. *A Two-Product Economy* — 122
    (1) Introduction
    (2) Two Factors with a Variable Distribution of Income
    (3) Three Factors with a Constant Distribution of Income

APPENDIX III. *Depreciation by Sudden Death* — 173

SUMMARY OF NOTATION USED — 184

CHAPTER 1

Introduction

The purpose of this book is limited. It is designed to show the way in which the simplest form of classical economic system would behave during a process of equilibrium growth. Until recently most classical systems have been designed to answer problems in comparative statics—that is to say, in order to compare two economies in static equilibrium which are identical except in one respect, so that the ultimate effect of this specified change in the basic conditions of the economy on the static equilibrium values of the other relevant variables can be examined. In this book an extremely simple classical model of an economic system will be examined in such a way as to observe the process of change in the variables over time instead of for the purposes of comparing two static positions.

No elaborate attempt will be made in this book to persuade the reader of the realism or utility of the very simplified classical economy here examined. But the author would in fact claim that this analysis has a real usefulness. There is presumably in any case some limited usefulness in bringing out the implications for economic growth of the type of classical analysis with which economists are all so familiar. It may, in the author's opinion, be argued further that in the social studies there is a special merit in continuity of tradition and method—that there is positive virtue in putting new wine in old bottles if the bottles are strong enough. And in this case, in the author's opinion, the bottles will stand the strain. An economy can grow for three reasons: first, because net savings are being made out of current income so that the stock of capital instruments of production is growing; second, because the working population is growing; and, third, because technical progress allows more and more output to be produced by a given amount of resources as time passes. There is nothing in the nature of things which prevents one from examining the way in which a classical model of an economic system (e.g. with perfect atomistic competition) would behave over time if real capital were being accumulated, the working population were growing, and technical progress were taking place. One can then subsequently attempt to bring the results nearer to reality by modifying the classical assumptions of this growing classical economy (e.g. by allowing for the effects of certain forms of imperfect competition). There is no reason in the author's opinion why this should prove to be an unprofitable procedure; but the purpose of this book is limited to the production of the model and does not attempt to demonstrate its utility.

What then are the basic assumptions upon which the model in this book is constructed? It will be assumed throughout that we are dealing with a closed economy without any economic or financial relationships with other economies; that there are no State or governmental economic activities involving taxation or State expenditure; and, unless it is stated to the contrary, that all economic activity is carried out in conditions of perfect competition (with its corollaries of prices equal to marginal costs and net factor rewards equal to the value of their marginal net products), and that there are constant returns to scale in the sense that if, in any given state of technical knowledge, all the factors of production in any one industry were increased by x per cent then the output would also be increased by x per cent.

We shall assume further that there are only two commodities produced in our economy, namely a consumption good and a capital good. The consumption good satisfies all ultimate human needs for food, clothing, shelter, etc., while the capital good is used as an instrument of production to assist the production of a further output of consumption goods or capital goods. The capital good is, therefore, both the output of one of our two industries and also an instrument of production used in both of our two industries. To ease the exposition, when we are thinking of the current output of the capital-good industry we shall talk of 'capital goods'; but when we are considering the stock of capital goods available at any moment of time to aid in the production of further output we shall talk of 'machines'. Machines constitute the only form of capital. Working capital in the form of goods in process of production is neglected. Besides machines there are two other factors of production in our economy, namely land and labour. We have then a certain amount of land, labour, and machines being used at any one time to produce a certain output

2

of consumption goods; and we have at the same time the remaining available amount of land, labour, and machines being used to produce a certain output of capital goods, which will themselves be being used to replenish the existing stock of machines.

We desire to watch this system grow through time as the existing stock of machines grows, as the size of the working population increases, and as technical progress raises productivity. But in this book we shall confine ourselves to watching this process of growth on the assumption that the growing system remains in equilibrium. We must explain at some length what is meant by this; and this explanation can perhaps best be made in terms of the monetary system which we shall be assuming.

Although we are assuming that there is no governmental budget —no taxation and no State expenditure—we are not assuming that there is no central monetary authority. On the contrary, we shall assume that there is a banking system with a central bank and that the rate of interest is thereby always set at such a level as to preserve a constant cost-of-living index, i.e. a constant money price of our single consumption good. The mechanism must be of the following type. If the price of the consumption good tends to fall, the rate of interest is lowered (or more generally the terms on which monetary funds can be acquired by our private entrepreneurs for expenditure on investment in new machines are eased) so as to increase the incomes of those producing capital goods and, through the multiplier, the incomes of those producing consumption goods to the degree necessary to increase monetary expenditure on consumption goods to the extent necessary to prevent any fall in their money price. This easing (or tightening) of monetary conditions must be imagined to be carried out with such foresight and precision that there is never in effect any appreciable fall (or rise) in the money price offered for a consumption good.

Against this background of a constant money selling price for the consumption good we assume that full employment of labour and land available at any one moment of time is achieved by the adjustment of the money wage per worker and the money rent per acre of land. The wage per worker is always low enough to give entrepreneurs (who are faced with a constant price at which they can sell the final product of labour) an incentive to employ the whole available labour force, and the wage per worker is never so low as to cause the demand for labour by entrepreneurs to exceed the available supply. And similarly with the money rent per acre. Once more we must assume that these adjustments of factor prices are carried out with perfect foresight and precision so that there is never any excess supply of, or excess demand for, labour or land[1].

We thus have in our model of equilibrium growth a constant money price of consumption goods and full employment of labour and land. Presumably we also need some similar assumption to ensure the continuous full employment of the available stock of our third factor, machines. But this is in fact already implied in our monetary assumptions. An entrepreneur will wish to employ another machine if the interest which he will have to pay on the employment of an additional machine is sufficiently below the profit which he can hope to earn on an additional machine. If in any given circumstances the rate of interest is set too high by the monetary authorities, entrepreneurs will have little or no incentive to invest in more machinery; and expenditure on investment in new machines will be zero or very low so that a deflation of money incomes and of the money price of consumption goods will not be avoided. On the other hand if the rate of interest is set too low by the monetary authorities, entrepreneurs will have an incentive not only to employ all the existing stock of machines, but also to add to their stock of machines at a very high rate; but this will involve an excessive level of expenditure on investment in new machines so that an inflation of the price of the consumption good would not be avoided. In other words if we assume that the money wage per worker and the money rent per acre are always at the level required to ensure full employment of labour and land and if we further assume that the rate of interest is set at a level which ensures that the flow of money expenditure on investment in new machines is sufficient to prevent any rise or fall in the money price of consumption goods, we are in effect also assuming that the existing stock of machines is fully employed.

If we are assuming that, no matter what the amount of land may be or how quickly the population is growing or the stock of machines is accumulated, there is always full employment of all

---

[1] These assumptions in fact mean that we are ignoring all the dynamic problems involved in ensuring that our economy does not leave the path of equilibrium growth.

available land, labour, and machinery, we are, of course, assuming that the production functions are such that one can in fact substitute one factor for another. It is possible in any given state of technical knowledge to produce our consumption good or our capital good by a more labour-intensive method (if labour is cheap and plentiful), by a more land-intensive method (if land is cheap and plentiful), or by a more machinery-intensive method (if machines are plentiful and cheap to hire)[1].

This is in fact a very realistic assumption. Different techniques are in fact used according to the price of the factors of production. But in the case of the substitutability between machines on the one hand and land and labour on the other hand we shall start by making an additional and very unrealistic assumption. In fact a machine is designed and built for a certain technique of production —a simple hand-loom if the hire of labour is very cheap and that of machinery is very expensive, but an elaborate automatic loom if the hire of labour is very expensive and that of machinery is very cheap. But once a particular machine is designed and built there are in fact often very narrow limits to the degree to which the amount of labour can be varied with that particular machine. In other words, in reality, machinery of a given cost can *in the long run* be designed in a form to be used with a large, or in a form to be used with a small, amount of labour; but *in the short run* it is not possible greatly to alter the amount of labour which can profitably be employed to operate a given machine.

We shall, however, start with the unreal but simple assumption that all machines are alike (they are simply a ton of steel) and that

---

[1] In much of what follows we shall speak of the wage per worker, the rent per acre, and the profit per machine as measuring the cost to the entrepreneur of hiring an additional worker, acre of land, or machine. In the case of machinery this use of words needs some explanation. We are dealing only with competitive equilibrium situations. In such conditions the profit per machine must be the same in all uses. If one entrepreneur uses an extra machine for one purpose, then the opportunity cost is the profit which is lost through not being able to use that machine for some other purpose; and in a fully competitive market by one means or another (either through the interest which must be paid on a loan to purchase the machine or the terms of hire or of hire-purchase of the machine or simply the alternative opportunity of profit foregone by the owner of the machine) this profit foregone from other uses of the machine will measure the cost to the entrepreneur of using the machine for this particular purpose. Thus if the profit per machine is low throughout the economy, the cost of using a machine for any particular purpose will be low.

the ratio of labour to machinery (i.e. of workers to tons of steel in stock) can be varied with equal ease in the short run as in the long run. We may call this *the assumption of perfect malleability of machinery*; for it is exactly as if a certain tonnage of steel which had been constructed into a machine of a given sort (i.e. suitable to produce one of our two products with the techniques expected to be the most appropriate for the state of technical knowledge and for the relative cost of the different factors of production) could at a moment's notice and without cost be remoulded into another form of machine suitable to produce whatever had turned out to be the most profitable product by whatever had turned out to be the most profitable technique. In fact, much the same sort of result would follow from the assumption of perfect f oresight, even if we did not assume that the capital good, once it had been installed in a particular form, could be readily remoulded into another form. In fact, what we are concerned with in this book is primarily to see how the economy would grow in equilibrium, i.e. in conditions in which *inter alia* the capital good has in all cases been wisely installed in its most appropriate forms for all the purposes for which it is being used.

Another assumption which we shall make at first is that the production function for a unit of the consumption good is at every moment of time the same as the production function for a unit of the capital good. This we may call *the assumption of perfect substitutability in production between capital goods and consumption goods*. The effect of this assumption is that, whatever may happen to technical knowledge, the cost-price of a machine is the same as the cost-price of a consumption good. In effect, this is equivalent to the assumption that in our economy only one commodity is produced which may be used either for final consumption or for additions to the stock of instruments of production. The economy produces cows which may be eaten as meat or used as instruments of production to produce more cows[1].

---

[1] The two-commodity economy to which we shall in due course revert is one in which cows are used as machines in rather different ways to produce meat to be eaten (consumption goods) and to produce more cows (capital goods) to be used as machines to produce meat or cows. If wages or rents changed and if farming to produce meat required a different amount of labour and land per cow than did farming to breed further cows, or if technical progress in producing meat was at a different rate than in breeding further cows, the cost-price of cows might vary in terms of meat.

We shall not assume that machines last for ever; but we shall assume at first a rather unrealistic form of depreciation of machinery, namely that of any given stock of machines, no matter how old or how new they are, a certain percentage collapses or disappears each year. Thus each year ten per cent, for example, of the existing stock of machines (measured in tons of steel) would need to be replaced, regardless of the time for which the existing machines had already been used. This we shall call *the assumption of depreciation by evaporation.* It has two simplifying effects in our model: in the first place, the value of the capital stock of machinery in our system is always equal to the amount of machinery in existence (e.g. the tonnage of steel in stock) multiplied by the cost price of a new machine (e.g. a newly produced ton of steel), an old ton of steel being just as valuable as a new ton of steel since of each the same proportion (e.g. ten per cent) will evaporate in any year; and, second, expenditure needed for the replacement of machinery will always be equal to the depreciation allowance which must be made in respect of the existing machinery —in the above example both being equal to ten per cent of the value of the capital stock of machinery.

At a later stage we shall discuss the effects on our system of modifying these three last assumptions (namely those of the perfect malleability of machinery, of perfect substitutability in production between capital goods and consumption goods, and of depreciation by evaporation); but we will start by setting our model to work on all these extreme simplifying assumptions.

CHAPTER 2

Three Determinants of the Rate of Economic Growth

So long as we maintain the assumption of perfect substitutability in production between capital goods and consumption goods (which we shall do until we reach Chapter 8 below), we are in fact dealing with a single-product economy, this product being useful for the two purposes of being consumed by consumers and being used by entrepreneurs as a man-made instrument of production or machine. In this case we can say that the net output produced by the economy (which will be available for consumption or for addition to the stock of machines) depends upon four things; first, the amount of the existing stock of machines (which will help to produce the gross output of the community but will also determine how much must be deducted from this gross output to maintain the stock of machines as they evaporate); second, the amount of labour available for productive employment; third, the amount of of land or natural resources available for productive use in the economy; and, fourth, the state of technical knowledge which we assume to be improving through time. We can write this simple relationship in the form of the following production function,

$$Y = F(K, L, N, t)$$

where $Y =$ net output or net real national income, $K =$ the existing stock of machines, $L =$ the amount of labour, $N =$ the amount of land, and $t =$ time, since the mere passage of time brings technical progress and allows Y to be raised even without any increase in K, L, or N.

As time passes three things can occur to cause Y to rise.

First, K, the stock of machines, may increase because the community is saving part of its income and is thereby accumulating real capital. Suppose that in the course of a year the stock of machinery goes up by an amount equal to ΔK. Then this itself will cause an increase in output equal to $V\Delta K$, where V is the marginal net physical product of a machine. V thus measures the increment of the community's annual output which would be caused by having one more machine to use, after deducting from the community's output the additional amount needed to meet the annual evaporation of the new machine. In our one-commodity economy (i.e. with the assumption of perfect substitutability between capital goods and consumption goods in production) this marginal product V has the dimensions of a rate of interest or a rate of profit. For example, suppose that to have one more machine in productive employment, everything else constant, would enable the community to increase its net annual output by 0·05 capital goods or consumption goods, then V would equal 5 per cent per annum. An increment of 100 machines in stock ($\Delta K = 100$) would enable net annual output to be permanently raised by five machines or its constant equivalent in consumption goods ($V\Delta K = 5$ per cent of $100 = 5$). What we have just said is true of any production function. But if in addition we assume constant returns to scale, perfect competition, and equilibrium growth, the owners of machines will earn on them a profit which is equal to the net marginal product of the machine. In this case V would also measure the equilibrium competitive rate of profit on capital[1].

Second, L, the working population, may grow. If in any one year the amount of labour productively employed were to rise by ΔL, then there would be for this reason alone an increase in the

---

[1] Thus if a machine costs £100 to install this year and a gross profit of £15 is made on it this year, from which £10 must be deducted to buy machinery to make up for this year's evaporation of the machine, the rate of profit as defined in the text is 5 per cent. So long as we maintain the assumptions of competitive equilibrium and the perfect malleability of machinery, the rate of profit as defined in the text must be the same for all uses of machinery at any one time. So long as we maintain the assumptions of competitive equilibrium and the perfect substitutability in production between consumption goods and capital goods, the price of a machine will (with a constant money price of consumption goods) be £100 next year as it was this year, so that there will be no capital gain on the machine and the rate of profit as defined in the text will measure the rate of yield on capital invested in machinery. But it is not assumed that this rate of profit will remain constant, nor that it is expected to remain constant, over future years. What the long-term rate of interest at which funds can be borrowed must be to prevent a monetary inflation or deflation in the general level of demand for machinery and so, through the multiplier, for consumption goods will, therefore, depend not only upon the current rate as defined in the text, but also upon expected future changes in that rate of profit.

community's output equal to $W\Delta L$, where W measures the marginal product of labour, which in constant-returns competitive equilibrium would also equal the real wage-rate paid to labour.

Third, we assume that the amount of land or natural resources available to the community is fixed, so that there is no change in N to affect the level of Y. But as time passes (as t grows), Y would rise even if K, L, and N remained unchanged, because growing technical knowledge would enable more to be produced by the same amount of the factors. Let us use the term $\Delta Y'$ to indicate the amount by which net output Y would rise in any one year because of technical progress, even if there were no change in the amount of machinery or in the working population.

Now if the changes which take place in any one year are not very great, we can assume that the total change in net output (which we will call ΔY) is equal to the sum of the three influences which we have just discussed separately. In other words

$$\Delta Y = V\Delta K + W\Delta L + \Delta Y'$$

or the increase over the year in the rate of annual net output (ΔY) is equal to the increase in the stock of machinery (ΔK) multiplied by its marginal product (V) plus the increase in the amount of labour (ΔL) multiplied by its marginal product (W) plus the increase in the rate of annual output due simply to technical progress ($\Delta Y'$). This basic relationship can be written

$$\frac{\Delta Y}{Y} = \frac{VK}{Y}\frac{\Delta K}{K} + \frac{WL}{Y}\frac{\Delta L}{L} + \frac{\Delta Y'}{Y}$$

where $\frac{\Delta Y}{Y}$ equals the annual proportionate rate of growth of output, $\frac{\Delta K}{K}$ the annual proportionate rate of growth of the stock of machinery, $\frac{\Delta L}{L}$ the annual proportionate rate of growth in the working population, and $\frac{\Delta Y'}{Y}$ the annual proportionate rate of growth of output due solely to technical progress, which we will call the rate of technical progress. Let us call these four pro-

portionate rates of growth y, k, l and r respectively[1]. $\dfrac{VK}{Y}$ is equal
to the proportion of the net national income which would be paid
in net profits, if the owners of machinery received a reward equal
to the value of the net marginal product of machinery; for K is
the amount of such machinery in use and V is the net marginal
product of a machine, so that VK is the total net profit which
would be received if each machine earned a net profit equal to
the value of its marginal net product and $\dfrac{VK}{Y}$ is, therefore, the
proportion of the net national income which would be paid in net
profits in these circumstances. $\dfrac{VK}{Y}$ also measures the elasticity of
the output (Y) in respect to changes in the use of the factor (K)[2].
Thus if $\dfrac{VK}{Y} = 0.6$, *either* we can say that if the owners of machines
received profits equal to their marginal net products, 60 per cent
of the net national income would go in profits, *or* we can say that
a 1 per cent increase in the amount of machinery in use would
cause a 0.6 of 1 per cent rise in output. These are two ways of
saying the same thing. We will write the proportion $\dfrac{VK}{Y}$ as U,
and we will call it the proportional marginal product of machinery.
In the special case of a constant-returns production function and
of competitive equilibrium it will be equal to the proportion of
the national income received in profits. Similarly, $\dfrac{WL}{Y}$, which we
will call Q, represents the proportional marginal product of labour
and would be equal to the proportion of the net national income
going to wages in the special case of a constant-returns competitive
equilibrium.

---

[1] These proportionate rates of growth have the same dimensions as a rate of
profit or a rate of increase. They are 10 per cent per annum or 1 per cent per
annum, for example. In what follows we shall call them growth rates to avoid
the clumsy phrase 'proportionate rates of growth'.

[2] V, the marginal product of K, is $\dfrac{\partial Y}{\partial K}$, so that $\dfrac{VK}{Y} = \dfrac{K}{Y} \cdot \dfrac{\partial Y}{\partial K}$ or the proportionate increase in Y divided by the proportionate increase in K.

We can, therefore, write our basic relationship as

$$y = Uk + Ql + r$$

which shows the growth rate of output (y) as being the weighted sum of three other growth rates, namely the sum of the growth rate in the stock of machines (k) weighted by the marginal importance of machinery in the productive process, i.e. in a competitive equilibrium by the proportion of the national income going to profits (U) *plus* the growth rate of the population (l) weighted by the marginal importance of labour in the productive process or, in a competitive equilibrium, by the proportion of income going to wages (Q) *plus* the growth rate of technical progress (r) .

We can write this basic relationship $y = Uk + Ql + r$ in the form:

$$y - l = Uk - (1 - Q)l + r.$$

Now $y - l$ is the difference between the growth rate of total output and the growth rate of the working population and it measures, therefore, approximately the growth rate of real income per head. For example, if total real income is rising by 10 per cent per annum but the working population is growing by 8 per cent per annum, income per head will be rising by (approximately) 2 per cent per annum. It is the growth rate in this real income per head in which we are presumably most interested. Our basic relationship says that the growth rate in real income per head ($y - l$) is the outcome of three factors: first, it is raised by the growth rate in real capital (k) weighted by its proportional marginal product or by the proportion of the net national income which would be paid to profits in a competitive equilibrium (U); second, it is depressed by the growth rate in the working population (l) weighted by one minus the proportional marginal product of labour ($1 - Q$); and, third, it is raised by the rate of technical progress (r). The second of these three elements (namely, $- [1 - Q]l$) which tends to depress the growth rate of real income per head is, of course, the familiar tendency for diminishing returns to labour to set in as more and more labour is applied to any given amount of land and capital equipment.

But does not classical economic analysis teach us that diminishing returns to labour may be offset by increasing returns to scale? May not the advantages of producing on a large scale as a result of having a large working population outweigh the disadvantages of having each worker less well equipped with natural resources and with man-made instruments of production? This is, of course, a possibility.

In order to examine this possibility in more detail, let us go back to the basic production function given on page 8 above, namely:

$$Y = F(K, L, N, t).$$

Consider the position at any one point of time (i.e. with t constant) and, therefore, with any one given state of technical knowledge. We ask the question by how much output now would be greater if there were now, in the present state of technical knowledge, different amounts of machinery, men, and natural resources available for production. We obtain the answer

$$\Delta Y = V\Delta K + W\Delta L + G\Delta N$$

or that the increase in output (ΔY) is equal to the increase in the amount of machinery (ΔK) multiplied by its marginal product (V) plus the increase in the amount of labour (ΔL) multiplied by its marginal product (W) plus the increase in the amount of land (ΔN) multiplied by its marginal product (G).

We can express this in proportional terms as

$$\frac{\Delta Y}{Y} = \frac{VK}{Y}\frac{\Delta K}{K} + \frac{WL}{Y}\frac{\Delta L}{L} + \frac{GN}{Y}\frac{\Delta N}{N}.$$

$\frac{VK}{Y}$ is the proportional marginal product of machinery or the amount of the national income which would go to profits if machines earned a reward equal to their marginal product, and let us, as before, call this U. Similarly, as before, we write $\frac{WL}{Y}$ as Q. And let us write $\frac{GN}{Y}$ (the proportional marginal product of land or the proportion of the national income which would be paid in ground-rent if land were paid a reward equal to the value of its marginal product) as Z. Then we have

$$\frac{\Delta Y}{Y} = U\frac{\Delta K}{K} + Q\frac{\Delta L}{L} + Z\frac{\Delta N}{N}.$$

Now it is a familiar proposition in classical economic analysis (which will not be expounded here) that a fully competitive equilibrium in which all factors of production are paid rewards equal to the value of their marginal social net products is possible only in conditions of constant returns to scale. If there are increasing returns to scale, either there will be elements of monopoly somewhere in the economy or else there will be elements of external economy which will mean that marginal social product exceeds marginal private product in some parts of the economic system. Closely allied to this familiar proposition is the proposition (which also will not be expounded here) that in conditions of constant returns to scale, the payment of a reward to each factor equal to its marginal product will absorb the whole, and neither more nor less than the whole, of the available product. In this case in the above equation

$$U+Q+Z = 1.$$

In other words, the sum of the proportions of the national income which would go to profits, wages, and rents would in this case add up to unity, i.e. would account for the whole of the national income. But it is a familiar proposition (which also will not be expounded here) that if there are increasing returns to scale in the economy, it is impossible to pay every factor a reward equal to the value of its marginal product because the payment of rewards on this principle would require more than the total available product; or, in other words, in the case of increasing returns to scale

$$U+Q+Z > 1.[1]$$

---

[1] For a demonstration of these propositions the reader is referred to J. E. Meade—Trade and Welfare, pp. 32–42. Their validity can, however, be indicated in terms of our present formula. Suppose that all three factors increased by 10 per cent (i.e. $\frac{\Delta K}{K} = \frac{\Delta L}{L} = \frac{\Delta N}{N} = 10$ per cent). Then the equation on page 13 would give

$$\frac{\Delta Y}{Y} = (U+Q+Z) \times \frac{10}{100}$$

If all factors increase by 10 per cent, there are constant returns to scale only if output increases also by 10 per cent; but $\frac{\Delta Y}{Y}$ will equal 10 per cent only if $U+Q+Z = 1$. If all factors increase by 10 per cent, there are increasing returns to scale only if output increases by more than 10 per cent; but $\frac{\Delta Y}{Y}$ will exceed 10 per cent only if $U+Q+Z > 1$.

In the light of this analysis let us once more consider our basic relationship

$$y - l = Uk - (1 - Q)_l + r.$$

If there are constant returns to scale and $U + Q + Z = 1$, Q is certainly less than unity, the term $-(1 - Q)l$ is certainly negative and the growth rate of real income per head $(y - l)$ is certainly depressed by a high rate of population growth (l). But if there are increasing returns to scale and $U + Q + Z > 1$, then all we know is that $Q > 1 - U - Z$. It is now possible that $Q > 1$. This is the more likely to be so, first, the more important are the increasing returns to scale (i.e. the more Q exceeds $1 - U - Z$) and, second, the smaller are the proportional marginal productivities of capital and land (i.e. the smaller are U and Z).

Let us then, by way of example, consider the factors which will make Z low. The extreme case is where land is so plentiful as to become a free good; there is so much available land that it is used so extensively that its marginal product is zero; no one can find any use for any more land. In this case Z is zero. Where land and machinery were both so plentiful as to approximate to free goods and where, at the same time, there were important economies of large-scale production, a higher growth rate of population would cause a higher growth rate in the standard of living.

But it should not be inferred from this that in all circumstances the more plentiful is land, the lower is Z. Z is not the marginal product of land, but the proportional marginal product of land, namely the percentage increase in output which would result from a 1 per cent increase in the amount of available land. This, as we have seen, is the same thing as the proportion of the national income which would be paid in rent if land were paid a reward equal to the value of its marginal product. Z can be low, i.e. the proportional importance of land in production at the margin can be small, for either of two sets of reasons. In the first place, land may be very plentiful (which would in itself tend to *raise* its proportional importance in production) but the substitutability between land and other factors in production may be so small (i.e. it may be so difficult to use land instead of labour or machinery to produce output) that its marginal product is so low that, in spite of the large amount of land, its proportional marginal product is low. The extreme case of this is the case which we have just examined, where land is a free good. But, secondly, in other conditions land might be proportionally marginally unimportant in production for the quite opposite reason that there was very little land available, but that technical methods were known whereby labour and machinery could easily take the place of land in production. The marginal product of land would now be fairly high because land was scarce; but the small amount of land would outweigh the height of its marginal product, and the proportion of the national income which would go to land if it were paid a rent equal to the value of its marginal product would be low. Thus Z will fall as the amount of land increases if the substitutability between land and other factors is small, but it will rise as the amount of land increases if the substitutability between land and other factors is great.

There is one very special but very simple case which is worth noting. Suppose that land were so plentiful as to be a free good, so that we need only consider the two factors, men and machinery. Suppose further that there were constant returns to scale. In this case the payment of profits equal to the marginal product of machinery and of wages equal to the marginal product of labour would just absorb the whole of the net national output, so that $Q+U = 1$. In this case

$$y-l = U(k-l)+r$$

so that the growth rate in real income per head $(y-l)$ would equal the growth rate in the amount of machinery per head $(k-l)$ weighted by the proportional marginal product of machinery (U) *plus* the rate of technical progress (r).

In our basic relationship $y-l = Uk-(1-Q)l+r$ the element Uk can be expressed in other forms. U, as we have seen, is $\dfrac{VK}{Y}$. k, the growth rate of the stock of machines, equals $\dfrac{SY}{K}$, where S is the proportion of the net national income which is saved; for SY will equal the amount of net real output which is added to the stock of machines in the course of a year so that $\dfrac{SY}{K}$ will equal the proportionate increase in the stock of machines over the year.

We have then $Uk = US\dfrac{Y}{K} = SV$, which expresses in three forms the same thing, namely the contribution which capital accumulation is making to the growth rate of final output. We can then express our basic relationship between the growth rate of real income per head and its three basic determinants in three different ways:

$$y - l = Uk - (1 - Q)l + r$$

$$y - l = US\frac{Y}{K} - (1 - Q)l + r$$

$$y - l = SV - (1 - Q)l + r.$$

These are all three ways of saying identically the same thing. In what follows we shall use whichever one of them is most convenient for the purpose in hand. But it may be useful to give a numerical example which the reader is advised to play with until familiarity breeds boredom, in order to see that these are but three ways of saying the same thing. Suppose that people saved 1/10 of their income ($S = 1/10$) and that the marginal product of real capital goods or the market rate of profit were 5 per cent per annum ($V = 5$ per cent per annum). Then the contribution of capital accumulation to the growth rate of output would be 1/2 per cent per annum. ($SV = 1/10$ of 5 per cent per annum $= 1/2$ per cent per annum.) The commonsense of this is obvious. If out of a year's income of 1000 people save 100 units of product ($S = 1/10$) and if a once-for-all addition of 100 units to the stock of machines increases annual output in every future year by 5 units ($V = 5$ per cent per annum), then the initial annual income of 1000 will be raised by this year's capital accumulation to 1005 or by 1/2 per cent in the course of the year ($SV = y = 1/2$ per cent per annum).

Suppose that, while the initial annual income was 1000 ($Y = 1000$), the initial stock of machines was 2000 ($K = 2000$). Then this same development could be expressed by saying that the stock of machines had gone up from 2000 to 2100 or by 5 per cent in the year

$$\left(k = \frac{SY}{K} = \frac{(1/10) \times 1000}{2000} \text{ p.a.} = 5\% \text{ p.a.} \right)$$

and that the proportion of the national income marginally due to the use of capital was $\frac{1}{10}$

$$\left(U = \frac{VK}{Y} = \frac{(5/100) \times 2000}{1000} = \frac{1}{10} \right)$$

so that the contribution of capital accumulation to the growth rate of final output was 1/10 of 5 per cent per annum or 1/2 per cent per annum ($Uk = 1/10 \times 5$ per cent per annum $= 1/2$ per cent per annum).

One can also see that the same result is obtained by multiplying together the proportion of the national income which goes to profits (U), the proportion of the national income which is saved (S), and the ratio of annual income to capital stock $\left(\frac{Y}{K} \right)$. For $US\frac{Y}{K}$ in our numerical example equals $1/10 \times 1/10 \times 1/2 = 1/2$ per cent per annum.

CHAPTER 3

Changes in the Rate of Economic Growth

We have now examined the main factors which will determine the growth rate of real income per head. We may now ask the question in what conditions the growth rate is likely itself to be rising or falling over time. Is growth likely to feed on itself and to become more and more rapid or is it likely to become less and less rapid and to peter out as the economy develops?

Consider our basic growth relationship in the forms

$$y = Uk+Ql+r \quad \text{and} \quad y = VS+Ql+r.$$

We shall treat l and r as exogenous variables which are determined for us by non-economic outside factors. In neither case is this assumption strictly realistic: the rate of population growth (l) may be affected by the level of, and the growth rate in, the standard of living ($y-l$); and the rate at which technical knowledge is improving (r) may be affected by the rate at which new machinery is being installed (k). However, for simplification, we shall assume that the growth rates of population and of technical knowledge (l and r) are given by external non-economic forces and are constant over time.

With l and r constant, whether y is rising depends upon whether $Uk(=VS)$ and Q are rising. In this Chapter we shall consider the forces which will be operating on these factors and so on y.

In order to consider these forces more precisely, we need a precise definition of the nature, as well as of the rate, of technical progress. The rate of technical progress we have already defined: suppose that in the course of a year technical knowledge so improves that, with an unchanged amount of land, labour, and machinery, 2 per cent more output could be produced, then we say that the rate of technical progress is 2 per cent per annum. But we also need a precise way of dealing with the possibility that the nature of the technical progress has been such as to be biassed in the direction of making labour (or land or machinery) especially more or less important for the productive process. The nature of technical progress in this respect is best measured by its effect upon the marginal product of the different factors. Thus, suppose that technical progress over the year would enable 2 per cent more to be produced by a given amount of land, labour, and machinery, but that it would raise the marginal product of labour in these circumstances by 3 per cent; then the technical progress can be said to be labour-using in character. It raises the average productivity of all factors by 2 per cent, but it raises the marginal product of labour by 3 per cent; it makes labour especially productive for use in additional amount. Conversely, if technical progress raised the marginal product of labour by less than the rate of technical progress itself, it can be said to be labour-saving in character. And similarly for the definition of technical progress of a land-using or land-saving or of a machinery-using or machinery-saving character.

A little reflection will show that we have now defined technical progress as labour-using or labour-saving according as it tends to raise or to lower the proportional marginal product of labour Q, as defined on page 11 above. As we there saw, $Q = \dfrac{WL}{Y}$ where W is the marginal product of labour, L the amount of labour, and Y the total national income. If, with a constant amount of all the factors including a constant amount of L, both the total product (Y) and the marginal product of labour (W) go up in the same proportion, then the proportional marginal product of labour or the proportion of the national income which would go to labour if labour were paid a reward equal to its marginal product (Q) would remain constant. If, however, technical progress raised W in a greater proportion than Y, technical progress would be labour-using by our definition and, with constant supplies of land, labour, and machinery, Q would rise. Similarly, labour-saving technical progress would tend to reduce Q[1], machinery-using technical progress would tend to raise U, machinery-saving technical progress would tend to lower U, land-using technical progress would tend to raise Z, and land-saving technical progress would tend to lower Z.

---

[1] In the sense that labour-saving technical progress would reduce Q if the total amount of land, labour, and machinery available for use in the economy remained unchanged.

As we have already seen (cf. page 14 above), if there are constant returns to scale $U + Q + Z = 1$, since in these conditions the payment of a reward to each factor equal to its marginal product absorbs the whole of the product, neither more nor less. It follows, that if there are constant returns to scale, technical progress (i) may be altogether neutral, i.e. may neither 'save' nor 'use' any factor, so that it tends to leave U, Q, and Z unchanged, or (ii) it it is biassed in the direction of 'saving' one factor it must simultaneously be biassed in the direction of 'using' another factor and *vice versa*, e.g. if it tends to lower Q it must tend to raise U or Z in an offsetting manner. Indeed, we can go further. Even if there are increasing returns to scale in the sense that the sum of $U + Q + Z$ is greater than unity, it is still true that technical progress if it is biassed in the direction of 'saving' one factor must be equally biassed in the direction of 'using' some other factor or factors, provided only that the degree of increasing returns to scale is constant in the sense that the sum of $U + Q + Z$ is constant.

But it is conceivable that technical progress is of a kind to make increasing returns to scale more (or less) important in the economy, in which case it is conceivable that, with our definitions, it could be biassed in the direction of 'using' or of 'saving' all factors at once; U, Q, and Z could all be raised, if at the same time their sum was raised. Thus suppose that in conditions in which large-scale production was unimportant technical progress took place in the form of the invention of new techniques for the best use of which larger-scale production was of great importance. Then with given initial small amounts of the factors the new knowledge might allow only a small increase in total output, because the initial amount of the factors could not make good use of the economies of large-scale. But it might enable large additions to production to be made by additional supplies of the factors. Thus, for example, the technical progress might be at a rate of only 1 per cent, in the sense that only a 1 per cent increase in output could be obtained from the existing factors, but it might raise the marginal product of every factor by 5 per cent; the technical progress would be simultaneously labour-using, land-using, and machine-using. It should, therefore, be remembered in what follows that, with our definitions, technical progress can only be biassed to 'use' one factor if it is simultaneously biassed to 'save' another factor, except in the special case where the technical progress itself affects the importance of the scale of production in reducing costs.

Having given these precise definitions of the nature, as well as of the amount, of technical progress, let us illustrate their use by considering for a moment the special case of economic growth where the population is constant. Real income per head grows (i) because of capital accumulation (there is more and more machinery available per worker and per acre of land) and (ii) because of technical progress. In what conditions will the interplay of these two factors cause the growth rate of the standard of living to accelerate or to decelerate?

In these conditions (i.e. with $l = 0$) our basic relationship showing the growth rate in the standard of living becomes

$$y = VS+r$$

so that, with a constant rate of technical progress (r), our problem boils down to the question whether VS will be rising or falling over time. This problem is illustrated by Diagram I on page 23. We measure on the vertical axis of that diagram the total annual net output (Y) and on the horizontal axis the total stock of machinery (K) in use to produce that output, the amounts of the other factors, land and labour, being constant. At any one time (i.e. with a given state of technical knowledge) we can draw a curve such as $F_1(K)$, which shows the amount of output (Y) which in the state of technical knowledge in year 1 would be produced by any given amount of machinery (K). If in year 1 the amount of machinery were OD, then the output in year 1 would be AD. The slope of the curve at A will measure the marginal product of machinery or (in our model in which the price of a machine is constant in terms of the price of other products) the rate of profit which would be earned on a machine if machine-owners received earnings equal to the marginal net product of machinery (V). For the slope of the F_1-curve at A measures the increment of output that would be produced by the use of one more unit of machinery in the current state of technical knowledge and with constant amounts of the other factors. We can assume also that because of diminishing returns to any one factor the slope of the F_1-curve becomes less and less steep as we move along it to the right, i.e. that the slope of the tangent at G is less steep than the slope of the tangent at A. At G we have OE instead of OD machinery applied to the same amount of land and labour in the same state of technical knowledge, and we can, therefore, assume that the marginal product of machinery will be lower.

Between year 1 and year 2 technical progress will have taken place. With any given amount of land, labour, and machinery we

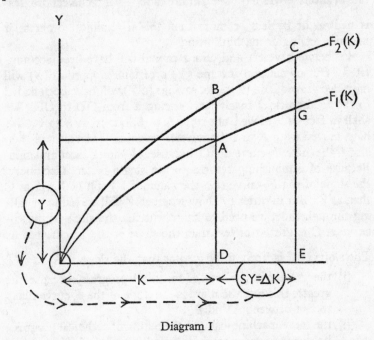

Diagram I

can produce more output. There will, therefore, be a new F-curve such that F_2 always lies above F_1; with the amount of machinery OD we could produce AD in year 1 but can produce BD in year 2. According to our definition the rate of technical progress (r) is equal to $\dfrac{AB}{AD}$, since this measures the proportionate increase in output produced by the initial amount of the factors, due to improved technical knowledge. With our definitions this technical progress will be machine-using (or machine-saving) if it raises the marginal product of machinery in a proportion which is greater (or less) than the rate of technical progress itself. In other words, if the technical progress is neutral in its effect on machinery, the slope of F_2 at B will be greater than the slope of

F_1 at A in the same proportion as the output BD is greater than the output AD. If the slope of the F-curve between A and B has risen by more than this, the technical progress is machine-using; if by less than this, it is machine-saving. Between A and B the rate of profit V will have risen in the ratio $\dfrac{BD}{AD}$ if technical progress is neutral or by less or more than this if technical progress is machine-saving or machine-using.

But between year 1 and year 2 capital will have been accumulated. Out of net real income (Y) a certain proportion (S) will have been saved, and these net savings (SY) will have been added to the total stock of machinery, raising it from OD to OE. We shall in fact have moved not from A to B, but from A to C. We have moved from A to B because of technical progress and then along the new F-curve to C because of capital accumulation. Because of diminishing returns to the single factor, machinery, the slope of the F_2-curve (i.e. the value of V) will be lower at C than at B. But in order to know whether V will be rising or falling through time, we need to know whether the slope of the F_2-curve at C is greater or less than the slope of the F_1-curve at A.

The slope at C is likely to be greater than the slope at A,

(i) the greater is the rate of technical progress, because the greater this rate the more is the slope of the F-curve likely to rise between A and B,

(ii) the more machine-using is the nature of technical progress, because the more machine-using is technical progress the more the slope of the F-curve will be raised between A and B,

(iii) the lower is the proportion of income which is saved (S), because the lower is S the less we shall move to the right along the F_2-curve and the less the slope of the F-curve will fall between B and C, and

(iv) the more readily machinery can be subsituted for land and labour in production, because the less the marginal importance of machinery in production falls simply because there is a greater amount of machinery in use per worker and per acre the smaller will be the fall in the slope of the F-curve as we move to the right along the F_2-curve from B to C as a result of capital accumulation.

If the proportion of income saved is constant, the four conditions (i) to (iv) above will determine whether or not the growth-rate of the national income will be rising or falling with the passage of time. We have seen that with a constant population (i.e. with $l = 0$), $y = VS + r$. It follows that with S and r also constant, y will be rising or falling according as V is rising or falling; and the four conditions (i) to (iv) above will therefore together determine whether y is rising or falling.

But let us now generalise the analysis and consider what determines whether the growth rate y will be rising or falling when we allow for the facts that the working population may be growing and that the proportion of income saved may be changing. The forces which will be at work affecting the growth rate of the national income may best be considered under four heads[1].

(1) The rate at which the national product will be growing will depend *inter alia* upon the rate at which the stock of machines is growing. Since $y = Uk + Ql + r$, anything which tends to raise the rate at which capital is being accumulated (k) will *ceteris paribus* raise the growth rate of the national product (y). Since $k = \dfrac{SY}{K}$, there are two things which will cause k to be rising over time: the first is a rise in the ratio of income to capital $\dfrac{(Y)}{K}$ and the second is a rise in the proportion of income saved (S). We will deal below with a rise in S. At present we are concerned with the conditions which will cause $\dfrac{Y}{K}$ to be rising. This will be the case if the rate of technical progress is high, the rate of population growth is high, and the proportion of income saved is low. If the proportion of income saved is low, K will be growing only slowly; and if the rate of technical progress and of population growth is high, Y will be growing rapidly even though K is growing slowly. Thus in these conditions $\dfrac{Y}{K}$ will be growing; therefore $\dfrac{SY}{K}$ or the rate of capital accumulation will tend to be

---

[1] These are considered in a more precise mathematical form in Section (2) of Appendix I (pages 100 to 108).

growing; and therefore the growth rate of the national product will itself tend to be growing.

(2) If S is itself growing, the rate of capital accumulation and so the growth rate of the national product will also tend to be growing. There are two main forces at work which may be causing S to rise or to fall with the passage of time.

First, S may change because real income per head from which savings can be made is itself changing. Suppose, for example, that population growth were low but that the rate of technical progress were high so that real income per head were rising. In such a case S might be rising because people were becoming richer and could save a larger proportion of their higher real incomes.

But, secondly, S might be rising because of a change in the distribution of income. Let us suppose that a larger proportion of rents and of profits than of wages is saved; then anything which causes a shift of income away from wages on to rents and profits would cause a rise in the proportion of income saved and thus a rise in the rate of capital accumulation and thus a rise in the growth rate of the national product. There are two sets of factors which might cause such a shift in the distribution of income.

(i) There would be a shift in the distribution of income away from wages if technical progress was of a labour-saving and of a capital-using or land-using kind; for in these circumstances technical progress would be increasing the demand for land and machinery relatively to labour.

(ii) The growth of population and of the stock of machinery will change the proportions in which these factors are used relatively to land and will probably change the proportion in which they are used relatively to each other. If the elasticity of substitution between labour and land is low, then the growth of population per acre will tend to lower the wage rate relatively to the rent of land very substantially and to shift income from wages to rents. If the capital stock is growing more rapidly than the population and the elasticity of substitution between men and machines is very high, then this will cause the profit per machine to fall very little relatively to the wage per worker and will cause a rise in total profits relatively to total wages. Alternatively, if the rate of population growth were greater than the rate of capital accumulation and the elasticity of substitution between men and machines were very low, this would cause a very substantial fall in the wage per worker relatively to the profit per machine, and once again total wages would fall relatively to total profits. In this way the rates of growth of population and of machinery relatively both to each other and also to the amount of available land may, in conjunction with the technical ease or difficulty of substituting the factor for another, cause profits and rents to rise relatively to wages and thus cause the proportion of income saved to rise, the rate of capital accumulation to rise, and the growth rate of the national product to increase.

(3) Suppose for a moment that a change in the distribution of income caused no change in the proportion of the national income which was saved and thus had no effect upon the rate of capital accumulation. There remains one way in which high elasticities of substitution between the factors of production will tend to cause the growth rate of the national product to be rising, while low elasticities of substitution between the factors will tend to cause the growth rate of the national product to be falling. This force will be operative provided only that some factors of production are growing or declining relatively to others. It makes no difference which factor is rising and which falling relatively to the other.

This important phenomenon can be understood best by considering the relationship $y = Uk + Ql + r$. A high elasticity of substitution between machinery on the one hand and labour and land on the other means that if k is very high and l very low, then U will be increasing rapidly while Q will be stagnant or falling. For as machinery increases, profit per machine will fall very little and the wage per worker and rent per acre will rise very little, so that the proportion of income going to profits (U) will rise and the proportion of income going to wages and rents (Q and Z) will fall. But U also represents the proportional marginal product of machinery and Q the proportional marginal product of labour. In other words, the factor which is increasing most rapidly (k) will be getting a larger and larger proportional weight at the margin (U) in causing a rate of growth of output (y). With a constant k and a rising U, y will itself be increasing. This will be partially but only partially offset by a falling Q because (i) part of the rise in U may be offset by a fall in Z so that the fall in Q is less than the rise in U and also (ii) because, even if the whole of the rise in U were matched by an equal fall in Q, Uk would be rising more rapidly than Ql was falling so long as k was greater than l—the simplest case being where the population as well as the acreage of land was constant so that Ql was zero.

Now it is to be observed that this argument would not be altered if the population were rising rapidly (l large) while the rate of capital accumulation were very small (k small). If all elasticities of substitution between the factors were high, Q would now be rising, U would be falling but by less than Q was rising, and l would be greater than k. Ql would, therefore, be rising more than Uk was falling and $Uk + Ql + r$ would therefore be rising.

We may call this the "to-him-that-hath-shall-be-given" situation; since the factor that is growing most rapidly acquires an ever-increasing proportionate productivity at the margin, it causes the growth rate of the national product continually to rise. In the opposite circumstances, that is to say if elasticities of substitution between the factors of production were very low, the most rapidly growing factors of production would acquire an ever decreasing importance at the margin and the growth rate of the national product would tend ever to decline.

(4) A very similar phenomenon may be caused by the nature of technical progress. Technical progress may happen to be such as to make the growing factors and more important at the margin. With r constant y will be rising if $Uk + Ql$ is rising. Technical progress may be changing U and Q. It is possible that it is causing both U and Q to rise. For with constant returns to scale $U + Q + Z = 1$, and both U and Q might be rising if Z were falling very quickly. In other words, inventions might be both capital-using and labour-using if they were simultaneously very land-saving. In this case with k and l constant, $Uk + Ql$ and so y would clearly be rising since both U and Q would be rising. If inventions were neither land-saving nor land-using (i.e. if Z were constant) Q would fall as usual as U rose and *vice versa*. But if, for example, inventions were equally capital-using and labour-saving, so that U rose as much as Q fell, $Uk + Ql$ and so y would nevertheless be rising if capital were being accumulated more rapidly than population was growing ($k > l$). The invention would be making capital more important and labour equally less important at the margin, and the high rate of capital accumulation relatively to population growth would therefore be causing a net increase in growth rate of the national product. In

general we can say that the nature of invention will be causing the growth rate of the national product to rise if it is causing U and/or Q to rise in such a way as to increase the weighted sum of U and Q, namely $Uk + Ql$.

To summarise, at any point in the process of economic growth, the growth rate of the national product and so (with a constant growth rate in the population) the growth rate in the standard of living will be tending to increase,

(1) if technical progress is so rapid as to be causing the ratio of income to capital to rise. For this in itself will be causing savings to rise relatively to the capital stock, and this rise in the rate of capital accumulation will tend to raise the rate of growth of the national product.

(2) if the nature of technical progress and the substitutability of the factors of production is such as to cause a shift of income towards those income recipients who save most. For this also will raise the rate of capital accumulation and so raise the rate of growth of the national product.

(3) if the elasticities of substitution between the factors of production are high. For this will tend to increase the importance at the margin of those factors which are growing most rapidly and so to raise the rate of growth of the national income.

(4) if the nature of technical progress itself is such as to increase the importance at the margin of those factors of production which are growing most rapidly.

CHAPTER 4

The State of Steady Economic Growth

Let us no longer assume that the population is constant, but return to our assumption that it is growing at a constant proportionate rate, l. We continue to assume that the rate of technical progress is constant. With a constant growth rate of population (l), the growth rate in income per head ($y - l$) will be constant only if the growth rate in total output (y) is constant. In this chapter we intend to examine a special case in which the growth rate in total output (y) and so the growth rate in income per head ($y - l$) is constant.

The object of this chapter is to show that if
  (i) all elasticities of substitution between the various factors are equal to unity,
 (ii) technical progress is neutral towards all factors, and
(iii) the proportions of profits saved, of wages saved, and of rents saved were all three constant,

then the growth rate of total output will in fact always move towards a given constant level, which represents a state of steady economic growth.

Conditions (i) and (ii) combined would mean that there was no change in the proportions of the national income which would be paid in profits and wages if machine-owners and workers received a reward equal to the value of their marginal products. U and Q would both be constant. Condition (ii) is simply the definition of technical progress of a kind which has no effect upon U and Q. Condition (i) requires a little more explanation.

If there are constant returns to scale and only two factors of production—say, machinery and labour—then the marginal product of each factor would depend solely upon the ratio of machinery to workers in the economy; and, because of diminishing returns to any one factor, the higher the amount of machinery per head, the lower would be the marginal product of yet another machine but the higher the marginal product of yet another worker. If machinery and men are very poor substitutes for each other and must be employed more or less in a fixed ratio, then this means that a rise in the amount of machinery per head will very quickly reduce the marginal product of machinery and will very quickly raise the marginal product of labour; a relatively small increase in the ratio of machines to men in employment will be sufficient to cause a given decline in the ratio of the marginal product of machinery to the marginal product of labour. The elasticity of substitution between machines and men could in these conditions be measured by the percentage increase in the ratio of machines to men which is necessary to bring about a 1 per cent decrease in the ratio of the marginal product of machinery to the marginal product of labour.

It follows that if the elasticity of substitution between machinery and men were equal to one, then any small changes in the supplies of machinery and of labour would leave the distribution of the national income between profits and wages unchanged. A 2 per cent rise in the amount of machinery per man would cause a 2 per cent rise in the ratio of total profits to total wages, if profits per machine and wages per worker remained unchanged; on the other hand, a 2 per cent fall in the ratio of the marginal product of machinery to that of labour (and so in the ratio of profits per machine to wages per worker) would cause the ratio of total profits to total wages to fall by 2 per cent, if the amounts of machinery and labour were unchanged. But if the elasticity of substitution were one, then a 2 per cent increase in the ratio of machines to men would be associated with a 2 per cent fall in the ratio of profits per machine to wages per worker; the former change would exactly offset the latter change and the distribution of income would remain unchanged. It can similarly be seen that according as the elasticity of substitution between machinery and men is greater (or less) than one, so an increase in the ratio of machinery to workers would cause a rise (or fall) in the ratio of total profits to total wages.

So much for an economic system with only two factors of production—machinery and men. But in our economy we have three factors of production—machinery, men, and land. In such a world the effects of changes in the supplies of machinery and men upon the distribution of the total national income between profits, wages, and rents depends upon three elasticities of substitution: (i) the elasticity of substitution between land and labour; (ii) that between land and machinery; and (iii) that between labour and machinery.

These elasticities of substitution need careful and precise definition. The best method of definition is of the following kind. The elasticity of substitution between labour and machinery is equal to the percentage increase in the ratio of machinery to labour which is needed to produce a 1 per cent decrease in the ratio of the marginal product of machinery to the marginal product of labour, when the amount of machinery is increased by a given small amount and the amount of labour decreased by just so much as is necessary to keep total output constant and when the amount of the third factor—land—is kept constant. Thus suppose that with a constant amount of land, a 1 per cent increase in the amount of machinery would just make good the loss of output due to a 2 per cent decrease in the amount of labour; but suppose that this increase in machinery and reduction in labour would reduce the marginal product of machinery by only 1/4 per cent and would raise the marginal product of labour by only 3/4 per cent. Then a 3 per cent increase in the ratio of machinery to labour would be associated with a 1 per cent decrease in the ratio of profits per machine to wages per worker, when the amount of land was kept constant, the adjustments in the amounts of machinery and labour being sufficient to keep output constant. The elasticity of substitution between machinery and labour would be as much as 3, this rather high figure marking the fact that machinery and men were rather good substitutes for each other because, although quite a large substitution was made of machinery for men in the production of a given amount of output in co-operation with a given amount of land, this did not greatly lower the marginal importance of machinery nor greatly raise the marginal importance of labour in production.

Now it is shown in Appendix I (but must be taken for granted here) that if there are constant returns to scale and if all three elasticities of substitution between our three factors land, labour, and machinery are equal to one, then no changes in the supplies of the factors of production will cause any change in the distribution of the national income between the three factors. All possible changes in the relative amounts of the factors would be compensated by opposite changes in the relative rates of reward to each factor.

It follows that conditions (i) and (ii) on page 30 above mean that the proportions of the national income going to profits, wages, and rents (namely, U, Q, and Z), will remain constant during the process of growth.

Now let S_v represent the proportion of profits which is saved. It follows that $S_v U Y$ represents the amount of profits which are saved, since UY is total profits and S_v is the proportion of profits which are saved. Similarly, $S_w Q Y$ and $S_g Z Y$ will represent the amounts of wages and of rents which are saved. But total savings are SY, where S is the proportion of the total national income which is saved. Since total savings equals the sum of the above three sources of savings we have

$$S = S_v U + S_w Q + S_g Z.$$

We have just seen that the result of conditions (i) and (ii) on page 30 is that U, Q, and Z are all constant. Condition (iii) on page 30 merely states that S_v, S_w, and S_g are all constant. It follows that S, the ratio of total savings to total national income will also be constant. The proportion of the national income saved (S) is the sum of the three constant proportions of profits, wages, and rents which are saved (S_v, S_w, and S_g), each respectively weighted by the constant proportion of the national income which goes to profits, wages, and rents (U, Q, and Z).

Now the rate of growth of output is given by our basic relationship

$$y = Uk + Ql + r$$

and y will be constant if and only if k is constant. For we are assuming that l and r are constant and, as we have just seen, conditions (i) and (ii) on page 30 mean that the proportional marginal products U and Q will be constant. It is, therefore, only if k is constant, that y will be constant.

But k, the growth rate of the capital stock, equals $\dfrac{SY}{K}$, since SY represents the amount annually added to the capital stock K through savings. But since, as we have just seen, conditions (i), (ii), and (iii) on page 30 mean that S is constant $\dfrac{SY}{K}$ or k will be constant, if and only if $\dfrac{Y}{K}$, the ratio of annual national income to the value of the capital stock, is constant. But $\dfrac{Y}{K}$ will be constant only if Y and K both grow at the same proportional rate per annum (the ratio of income to capital will be unchanged if both rise by, say, 5 per cent in the course of the year); or, in other words, $\dfrac{Y}{K}$ will be constant if $y = k$.

We have thus reached the conclusion that if the growth rate of the capital stock is equal to the growth rate of the national income, then the growth rate of income will be constant. The argument can be briefly recapitulated as follows. If the growth rate of the capital stock is equal to the growth rate of the national income (i.e. if $y = k$), then the ratio of the national income to the capital stock will be constant (i.e. $\dfrac{Y}{K}$ will be constant). Since the proportion of income saved is also constant (i.e. S is constant because S_v, S_w, S_g, U, Q, and Z are constant), the growth rate of the capital stock will be constant (i.e. $\dfrac{SY}{K} \equiv k$ is constant if S and $\dfrac{Y}{K}$ are both constant). But if the growth rate of the capital stock is constant, then the growth rate of the national income will be constant (i.e. $y = Uk + Ql + r$ will be constant if k is constant, because U, Q, l, and r are all constant).

In order, therefore, to understand the conditions in which the growth rate of income will be constant we have to investigate simply the conditions in which the growth rate of the capital stock will be equal to the growth rate of the national income. Consider again our basic relationship

$$y = Uk + Ql + r$$

in terms of a numerical example. Suppose $r = 1$ per cent per annum, $l = 2$ per cent per annum, $Q = 1/2$ and $U = 1/4$. Then the national output will in any case be growing by 1 per cent per annum because of technical progress ($r = 1$ per cent per annum) and by 1 per cent per annum because of the growth of the population ($Ql = 1$ per cent per annum), or by 2 per cent per annum for these two reasons combined. How fast the national income will be growing depends now upon the growth rate in the capital stock. If the capital stock were growing at 1 per cent per annum, the growth rate of the national income would be $2\frac{1}{4}$ per cent per annum, $\frac{1}{4}$ per cent per annum being due to capital accumulation ($Uk = \frac{1}{4}$ per cent per annum) and 2 per cent per annum due to population growth and technical progress; the growth rate of the national income would be greater than the growth rate of the capital stock. If the capital stock were growing very quickly at, say, 100 per cent per annum, the growth rate of the national income would be 27 per cent per annum, 25 per cent per annum because of the accumulation of capital ($Uk = \frac{1}{4} \times 100$ per cent per annum = 25 per cent per annum) and 2 per cent per annum because of population growth and technical progress; the growth rate of the national income would be below the growth rate of the capital stock. Somewhere in between there is a level of the growth rate of the capital stock which will make the growth rate of the national output equal to the growth rate of the capital stock. In our numerical example, a growth rate in the capital stock of $2\frac{2}{3}$ per cent per annum will have this effect, since $\frac{1}{4} \times 2\frac{2}{3} + +\frac{1}{2} \times 2 + 1 = 2\frac{2}{3}$.

It is, of course, very simple to derive this algebraically from our basic growth relationship. Suppose that the critical growth rate of the capital stock which makes the growth rate of output equal to the growth rate of the capital stock to be a, then we can write our basic relationship in the form

$$a = Ua + Ql + r$$

or

$$a = \frac{Ql + r}{1 - U}$$

In other words, if the growth rate of the capital stock is $\frac{Ql+r}{1-U}$, then the growth rate of the national income will also be $\frac{Ql+r}{1-U}$; and, in accordance with the argument on pages 33 and 34 above the growth rate of the national output will then be constant at this level.

Now the growth rate of the capital stock will initially be at this critical level of $\frac{Ql+r}{1-U}$ only if by a mere fluke of chance the thriftiness of various recipients of income happens to be just such as to

35

provide just those savings which are required to make the existing stock of capital accumulate at the rate $\frac{Ql+r}{1-U}$. What will happen if, for example, thriftiness were initially greater than this so that the rate of accumulation of the capital stock (which is equal to $\frac{SY}{K}$) were greater than the critical level? We should now have

$$\frac{SY}{K} > \frac{Ql+r}{1-U}.$$

Since $\frac{Ql+r}{1-U}$ is, as we have seen, the rate of accumulation of capital which will cause income (Y) and capital stock (K) to grow at the same proportionate rate, a rate of accumulation of capital greater than this critical rate will cause the capital stock (K) to grow at a greater proportionate rate than income (Y)[1]. So long, therefore, as $\frac{SY}{K} > \frac{Ql+r}{1-U}$, Y will be growing at a lower proportionate rate than K, $\frac{Y}{K}$ will be falling, and with S constant $\frac{SY}{K}$ will be falling. In other words if k starts above the critical steady-growth level of $\frac{Ql+r}{1-U}$, the capital stock will grow more rapidly than income; and, as savings grow only in proportion to income, the ratio of savings to the capital stock or the growth rate of capital will be falling towards the critical level $\frac{Ql+r}{1-U}$.

It could similarly be shown that if k started at a figure below the critical steady-growth level of $\frac{Ql+r}{1-U}$, then income would grow more quickly than capital, so that savings would grow more quickly than the capital stock and the rate of growth of the capital stock would in consequence rise towards the critical level $\frac{Ql+r}{1-U}$.

We may, therefore, conclude that if the growth rate of the

---

[1] An increase in k above the critical level a by say x will, as can be seen from our basic relationship $y = Uk + Ql + r$, raise y above the critical level a by only a fraction U of x.

population were constant, if the three elasticities of substitution between the three factors land, labour, and machinery were all unity, if technical progress were at a constant rate and neutral towards all factors, and if the proportions of profits, of wages, and of rents saved were all three constant, then the growth rates of real income and of the stock of machinery would both tend towards a constant level equal to $\dfrac{Ql+r}{1-U}$.

The basic argument of the preceding pages can be expressed by means of a simple geometrical construction. In Diagram II measure k, the growth rate of the stock of machinery, along the horizontal axis and y, the growth rate of the national income, up the vertical axis.

Through the origin O draw the line OCG with a slope such that $\dfrac{CD}{OD} = \dfrac{GH}{OH} = U$, the proportional marginal product of machinery. The height of this line then represents that part of

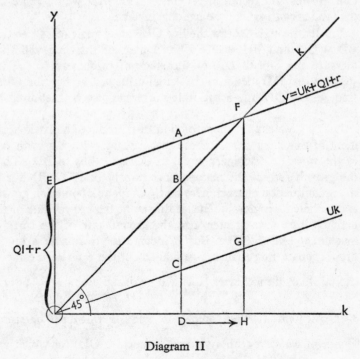

Diagram II

37

the growth rate of the national income which is due to the growth of the stock of machinery. For example, suppose that OD represented a growth rate of the stock of machinery of 6 per cent per annum and that U was $\frac{1}{3}$. Then CD would be 2 per cent per annum and this would represent the growth rate of the national income which was brought about simply by the growth in the stock of machinery.

Next measure up the vertical axis a length OE equal to $Ql+r$. This represents the growth rate of the national income which is due to the growth of population and to technical progress. Draw through E the line EAF, parallel to OCG. The height of the line EAF will then represent the total growth rate of the national income. Thus if OD was the actual growth rate of the stock of machinery, CD($= Uk$) would represent that part of the growth rate of the national income which was due to the accumulation of machinery and AC($=$ OE $= Ql+r$) would represent that part of the growth rate of the national income which was due to population growth and technical progress. Thus AD would represent the total growth rate of the national income.

Finally through O draw the line OBF at an angle of $45°$, so that BD = OD and FH = OH. The height of this line will then measure the growth rate of the stock of machinery (k). Thus suppose that OD measures the actual value of k at any time; then since BD = OD, the actual value of k can also be measured by BD.

Let us now use this construction to reproduce the basic argument of this chapter. Suppose that we start with a growth rate of the stock of machinery equal to OD and thus to BD. Then the growth rate of the national income will be AD (CD due to the accumulation of machinery and AC due to population growth and technical progress). But at this point the growth rate of the national income is greater than the growth rate of the stock of machinery (AD > BD). But if income is growing at a higher proportionate rate than the capital stock, the ratio of income to capital stock of machinery $\left(\dfrac{Y}{K}\right)$ will be rising. But $k = \dfrac{SY}{K}$, where S is constant. If, therefore, $\dfrac{Y}{K}$ is rising, k will itself be rising. Hence, if we start with a value of k (such as OD) for which y is greater than k ($AD > BD$), then k will be growing (i.e. the point D will be moving to the right along the horizontal axis). And this must go on until the point D coincides with the point H, at which point y is equal to k (both being equal to FH), so that $\dfrac{Y}{K}$ is constant, so that k which is equal to $\dfrac{SY}{K}$ will also be constant.

By a similar process of reasoning it could be shown that if we started with a value of k greater than OH, k would be greater than y, so that $\dfrac{Y}{K}$ would be falling, so that k which is equal to $\dfrac{SY}{K}$ would also be falling. The point F represents the state of steady growth at which $y = k$. Since GH $= Uk$ and FH is equal to k, FG must be equal to $(1-U)k$. But FG $=$ OE $= Ql+r$. Therefore, at the point F, $(1-U)k = Ql+r$ or $k = \dfrac{Ql+r}{1-U}$. This is the value which y and k will both have in the state of steady economic growth.

In Section (3) of Appendix I (pages 108 to 110) we consider in precise mathematical form the paths which Y, K, y, and k will all take over time, if we start from a state of affairs in which k is initially above or below the level of $\dfrac{Ql+r}{1-U}$, the rate at which it will finally come to rest in the state of steady growth. Suppose that we start from a state of affairs in which, given the initial stock of capital K_0 and so the initial level of income Y_0, the proportion of income saved was so great that $\dfrac{SY_0}{K_0}$ (which equals k_0 the initial rate of capital accumulation) was greater than its steady growth value of $\dfrac{Ql+r}{1-U}$. This state of affairs is represented in Diagram III which shows k_0 above $\dfrac{Ql+r}{1-U}$ and indicates how (in accordance with the formula given on page 110 of Appendix I) k would then fall towards this steady-growth rate of $\dfrac{Ql+r}{1-U}$. Uk will, of course, at every point of time be a constant proportion U of k, and y at every point of time will equal Uk plus the constant

39

figure $Ql + r$. The diagram shows how y and k will thus both fall until they converge at the value $\dfrac{Ql + r}{1 - U}$. The Appendix (pages 108 to 110) also shows what movements in the total capital stock K and the total national income Y are implied by these movements in the rate of capital accumulation k and the rate of growth of income y over time, starting from the initial capital stock K_0 and consequential initial income Y_0.

Here it is necessary only to emphasise the fact that these time paths of Y, K, y, and k are all paths of equilibrium growth in the sense that we have assumed that throughout the process full employment of all factors—machinery, labour, and land—is constantly maintained. We have thus two distinct types of equilibrium growth: (i) the state of steady growth which will be attained to the right of Diagram III and (ii) the equilibrium process of a changing rate of growth on the left-hand part of the diagram, a process of approach to the steady rate of growth if initial conditions $\left(\dfrac{SY_0}{K_0} \neq \dfrac{Ql + r}{1 - U} \right)$ are incompatible with a steady rate of growth.

We have confined ourselves in this book to an examination of equilibrium paths of growth by assuming (i) that there is a monetary policy which is completely and instantaneously effective in adjusting the level of investment (i.e. the level of expenditure on capital goods) to that which is necessary to maintain a constant demand price for consumption goods and (ii) that the money wage rate and the money rent of land is instantaneously and effectively adjusted to the level necessary to give full employment of labour and land at the constant money selling price of the final products of industry. Of course, in fact these adjustments will be imperfect and will take time. The introduction of these market adjustment processes would in fact lead to divergences of the time paths of Y, K, y, and k from those examined in Section 2 of Appendix I and displayed on Diagram III. We would then have a full unified theory of growth trends and of business fluctuations away from these equilibrium growth paths. There are, therefore, three stages of equilibrium and disequilibrium to bear in mind: (i) the final equilibrium state of steady growth, (ii) the equilibrium path of adjustment to this state of steady growth, and

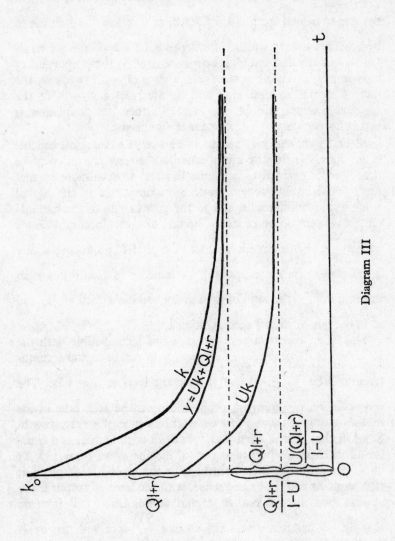

Diagram III

(iii) the disequilibrium fluctuations away from, or around, these equilibrium paths.

We have seen how, when the state of steady growth is reached, the rate of capital accumulation k will be equal to $\frac{Ql+r}{1-U}$. It is to be observed that this value of k depends only upon the constants Q, U, l, and r and is quite independent of S, the proportion of income saved. In other words, in a state of steady growth, the rate of capital accumulation and so the rate of growth of the national product will be the same whether the population is saving 15 per cent or 20 per cent of its income.

At first sight this may appear to be a most paradoxical conclusion. Surely if, in any given conditions at any one moment of time, people decided to consume less and to save more so that more could be invested, the rate of accumulation of the capital stock would be increased and so the growth rate of the national output would also be raised. The rate of capital accumulation k equals $\frac{SY}{K}$. With any given stock of capital K producing at any given time a certain output Y, an increase in S will cause an increase in $\frac{SY}{K}$ (the ratio of total savings to the capital stock) and so in the rate of capital accumulation k.

This is, of course, true. But it is not incompatible with the statement that *in a state of steady growth* the rate of capital accumulation will be $\frac{Ql+r}{1-U}$, no matter what the level of S may be. The reconciliation of these two propositions can be seen best in the following way. Suppose that we start in a state of steady growth. Suppose then that at a particular moment of time there is a once-for-all increase in the proportion of income saved from, say, 15 to 20 per cent. At that moment with the capital stock given at that moment and, in consequence, with the level of output given at that moment the rate of capital accumulation will increase sharply. S has increased by $\frac{1}{3}$ so that $\frac{SY}{K}$ or k will rise by $\frac{1}{3}$. But we shall now no longer be in a state of steady growth. In Diagram II the point D will have moved out to the right of the steady-state point H and k will be greater than y. In Diagram III

k will suddenly have risen to the point k_0 on the left of the diagram above its steady state level $\dfrac{Ql+r}{1-U}$.

The economy will now start on the process of adjustment back to the state of steady growth. The growth rate of the capital stock k will for the time being be greater than the growth rate of output and income y; the ratio of output and income to capital will be falling; and as a result of this fall in $\dfrac{Y}{K}$ the ratio $\dfrac{SY}{K}$—which rose above the steady state level of $\dfrac{Ql+r}{1-U}$ because of the once-for-all rise in S—will fall back towards the steady-state level. When it reaches this level again we shall be back in a state of steady growth; $\dfrac{SY}{K}$ once again will equal $\dfrac{Ql+r}{1-U}$; and if S is $\frac{1}{3}$ higher than it was before, $\dfrac{Y}{K}$ will be $\frac{1}{3}$ lower.

After the once-for-all rise in S, the level of K will at every moment in the future be greater than it would otherwise have been (more capital will have been accumulated); the level of Y will at every moment in the future be greater than it would otherwise have been (more output can at each future moment be produced because there will be a greater supply of capital equipment); and $\dfrac{Y}{K}$ will be lower than it otherwise would have been (because diminishing returns to capital will have caused the proportionate increase in output due to the larger capital stock to be smaller than the proportionate increase in the capital stock itself); and when $\dfrac{Y}{K}$ has fallen by as much as S rose, $\dfrac{SY}{K}$ will have regained its old steady-growth level of $\dfrac{Ql+r}{1-U}$.

This process is illustrated in Diagram IV for the special case in which the population is constant. Diagram IV is drawn on the same principle as Diagram I. We measure along the horizontal axis the stock of capital K, and up the vertical axis the amount of output Y which can be produced with any stock of capital K and with the given and constant amounts of labour and land.

This relationship between K and its output Y varies as time goes on because of technical progress. At year o the relationship is shown by the line $F_0(K)$, at year 10 by the line $F_{10}(K)$, and so on. Any F line slopes upwards because a larger K will produce a

Diagram IV

larger Y; the slope of an F line at any point represents the marginal product of K, i.e. the increase in Y which at that time would result if K had been one unit larger; and the slope of an F line flattens as one moves to the right because the marginal product of capital falls as more capital is applied to the constant amount of land and labour.

Consider now the lines α and β. We know that in a state of steady growth (with population constant so that $l = 0$) $\dfrac{SY}{K} = \dfrac{r}{1 - U}$ or $\dfrac{Y}{K} = \dfrac{r}{S(1-U)}$. Suppose that we are comparing two levels of S, a lower level S_a and a higher level S_b. Then in situation (a)

44

$\dfrac{Y}{K} = \dfrac{r}{S_a(1-U)}$ and in situation (b) $\dfrac{Y}{K} = \dfrac{r}{S_b(1-U)}$. Draw the line α through the origin O with the slope $\dfrac{r}{S_a(1-U)}$ and the line β through the origin O with the slope $\dfrac{r}{S_b(1-U)}$. Then with the lower proportion of income saved, S_a, the path of steady growth will be along the line from A_0 at year 0 to A_{10} at year 10, and so on. With the higher proportion of income saved, S_b, the path of growth will be along the line β from B_0 to B_{10} and so on. But in both cases the movement along the lines α and β will be at the same rate, namely $\dfrac{r}{1-U}$.

Suppose that the economy is moving along the line α, but that at year 0 there is a once-for-all increase of S from S_a to S_b. For the time being the economy will not move along a steady-growth line, but $\dfrac{Y}{K}$ will, as we have seen, be falling. The economy will move along some path like that shown by the heavy line in Diagram IV. Let us suppose that by year 10, however, it will for practical purposes have reached the new path of steady growth, namely the line β. The economy will now be at the point B_{10} instead of the point A_{10} at which it would have been if S had remained unchanged at the level S_a. Output will be $B_{10}C_{10}$ greater and the capital stock $A_{10}C_{10}$ greater than it would have been. Next year, the economy will be at B_{11} instead of A_{11} output will be $B_{11}C_{11}$ greater and the capital stock $A_{11}C_{11}$ greater than it would have been. Thus at every future point of time output, capital, and the ratio of capital stock to output will be greater than they would have been if the proportion of income saved had been unchanged. But the growth rates of output and of capital stock will have reverted to the previous level of $\dfrac{r}{1-U}$.

So far in this chapter we have been considering the value of y, the growth rate in the total national income. Let us close the chapter by turning to a consideration of the value of $y-l$, the growth rate in the level of income per head. From our basic relationship $y = Uk + Ql + r$ we can derive $y - l = Uk - (1-Q)l + r$

or $y-l = U(k-l)-Zl+r$. This states that as a general proposition, whether we are in a state of steady growth or not, the rate of growth of income per head will be equal to the rate of growth of capital per head $(k-l)$ multiplied by the marginal importance of capital in production (U) *minus* the rate of growth of population per constant acreage of land (l) multiplied by the marginal importance of land in the productive process (Z) *plus* the rate of technical progress (r). Technical progress will, of course, always help to raise output per head; the element $U(k-l)$ will be raising output per head provided that capital is being accumulated more quickly than population is growing; but the element Zl which measures the pressure of population upon the constant amount of land will always be tending to reduce the growth rate of output per head.

If now we make the assumptions necessary to lead to a state of steady growth (namely, unitary elasticities of substitution between the factors of production and neutral technical progress), we shall, as we have seen above (pages 35 to 39), approach the situation in which $y = k$ so that $y-l = k-l$. If we put this value of $k-l$ in the formula for $y-l$ given in the previous paragraph, we get

$$y-l = \frac{r - Zl}{1 - U}$$

which measures the rate of growth of income per head in the state of steady growth. Whether income per head is rising or falling will depend upon the balance between technical progress (r) and the pressure of population growth upon the land (Zl). If the rate of population growth l is $> \dfrac{r}{Z}$, there will be a steady rate of decline in the standard of living.

CHAPTER 5

The Overpopulated Economy

Up to this point we have used our analysis to determine what will be the rate of growth of total income and of income per head in an economy in which full employment of all factors of production is maintained. This has involved *inter alia* the assumption that the real wage rate is continuously adjusted to that level which is compatible with full employment, i.e. to the level equal to the marginal product of labour given all the other surrounding conditions. We have suggested (see pages 3 and 4) as a possible mechanism for the fulfilment of this assumption a state of affairs in which (1) monetary policy operates with unlimited foresight and effectiveness and keeps expenditure on capital development and so, through the multiplier, on consumption at the level necessary to maintain a constant money selling price for consumption goods and (2) the money wage rate is adjusted with unlimited fore sight and precision so as to give competitive employers at every moment of time an incentive to employ the total available working population—neither more no less.

Now there may be a totally different situation in the labour market with which our system can be readily adapted to deal. Consider an economy in which there was a very excessive population relatively to the amount of land and machinery available at any one time. Full employment of labour might involve so high a ratio of labour to land and machinery that the marginal product of labour was zero or even a negative quantity. Nothing could be added to output by employing more than a certain fraction of the available population. In such circumstances the real wage rate would not in fact be zero or negative; men would demand something for their labour, which we may call the subsistence wage. Only part of the population would be employed. The remainder would constitute a large reserve of unemployed labour available at the existing subsistence wage.

In such circumstances we would be interested in a different set of questions. We should, for example, be asking how quickly the demand for labour at the existing wage rate would be growing in given conditions of savings (and so of capital accumulation) and of technical progress rather than how quickly output would be growing if there were full employment of the total labour supply which was increasing at a given rate in given conditions of savings and of technical progress.

One simple change in the assumptions of our system is sufficient to apply the old analysis to our new set of problems. We can still assume that there is a monetary policy which so adjusts total money demand as to keep the selling price of consumption goods (i.e. the cost of living) constant; but whereas before we assumed that the money wage rate was continuously adjusted to give full employment to a population whose growth was determined by external demographic factors, we now assume that the money wage rate is fixed at a constant level, thus—with the constant cost of living—giving a constant real wage rate. In the previous analysis the rate of growth of employment was given, and one of the questions we had to answer was what would happen to the real wage rate; now the real wage rate is given and one of the questions to answer is what will happen to the amount of labour in employment.

This new application of the system is made in precise mathematical terms in Section (5) of Appendix I (pages 113 to 121). In this chapter we will confine ourselves to the rather more general statements that can be made without mathematical analysis. It is easy to see in general terms the three main sets of consideration which will now determine l, the growth rate in the demand for labour for employment.

(1) First, the greater is k at any one moment of time, the greater will l be. Capital accumulation with the given volume of employment would tend to raise the marginal product of labour and thus the demand for labour for employment. The greater, therefore, is k, the greater will be the rate of growth in the demand for labour. Starting at any given point with a given stock of machinery K_0 with a given and constant amount of land N, and with a given state of technical knowledge, there will be a given volume of employment which will bring the marginal product of labour into equality with the fixed real wage rate. These amounts of machinery, land, and labour will produce a given output Y_0. The rate of capital accumulation will be $\dfrac{SY_0}{K_0}$. We can, therefore,

say that starting at any point of time with a given capital stock K_0, the rate of growth in the demand for labour will be higher, the higher is the proportion of income saved, S.

(2) A second factor which may tend continually to raise the demand for labour is technical progress. (i) A higher rate of technical progress, and (ii) a bias in technical progress in a labour-using direction will both raise the marginal product of any given amount of labour employed with a given amount of land and machinery. At a constant real wage rate more labour will, therefore, be demanded for employment with any given supply of the other factors. Thus the higher and the more labour-using is technical progress, the more rapid will be the growth rate in the amount of labour in employment.

(3) Against these two factors increasing the demand for labour there may be a third factor tending to damp down the increase in the demand for labour. If there is a fixed amount of land and if land is a very important factor of production in the economy for which machinery and labour are bad substitutes, a relatively small increase in the volume of employment will serve to pull down again to the constant subsistence level any wage rate which has been raised above that level by capital accumulation or by technical progress.

Such in general terms are the three sets of factors at work in determining the growth rate of the volume of employment. In order to illustrate their mode of operation let us consider one or two special cases. In all these cases we shall assume that there are constant returns to scale and that the proportion of income saved is constant.

Case (i). Let us suppose that there are only two factors of production, labour and machinery, and that there is no technical progress. In this case it is easy to understand that employment, the stock of machines, and output will all grow at the same steady rate continuously.

The reason for this is straightforward. Suppose that in any year the stock of machines is increased by 2 per cent ($k = 2$ per cent p.a.). Then with constant returns to scale, no third limiting factor, and no technical progress, there can be a 2 per cent increase in the amount of labour employed ($l = 2$ per cent) without any change in the real wage rate; for in these conditions the marginal product of labour will remain unchanged only if the ratio of labour to capital employed is unchanged. But if labour and capital both increase by 2 per cent, then in these conditions output will also rise by 2 per cent ($y = 2$ per cent). In other words, $y = l = k$.

Moreover, it is easy to see that this common growth rate for Y, L, and K will also be a steady rate. Consider any initial position with a stock of machines K_0. Then with given technical conditions and no third factor, there will be a determinate amount of labour, L_0, which can be employed with K_0 at the given subsistence wage rate W_S. These amounts of labour and capital, L_0 and K_0, will produce a determinate amount of output Y_0. The rate of capital accumulation will then be determined by the level of the proportion of income saved, S, and will be equal to $\dfrac{SY_0}{K_0}$. But this means that in the second year the stock of capital will have risen to $K_0\left(1 + \dfrac{SY_0}{K_0}\right)$; and by the process of reasoning of the previous paragraph L_0 will also have risen to $L_0\left(1 + \dfrac{SY_0}{K_0}\right)$ and Y_0 to $Y_0\left(1 + \dfrac{SY_0}{K_0}\right)$. But since K and Y have both risen by the same proportion, $\dfrac{Y}{K}$ will be unchanged. Therefore, $\dfrac{SY}{K}$ will have remained unchanged at $\dfrac{SY_0}{K_0}$. In other words, k will remain unchanged at the steady-growth rate $\dfrac{SY_0}{K_0}$ and y and l will also both remain unchanged at this rate.

If the total population of working age is for demographic reasons growing at a lower rate than $\dfrac{SY_0}{K_0}$, the initial volume of unemployment will be falling relatively to the total employable population; but if the rate of population growth is greater than $\dfrac{SY_0}{K_0}$, the unemployment percentage will be rising.

Case (ii). Let us next suppose that there is a third limiting factor, land, but that there is no technical progress. With capital accumulation and growth in the volume of employment we are moving along an unchanged production function, but with a constant amount of the third factor land. In this case it is easy to see that the growth rate of output (y) must be less than the growth rate of the stock of machinery (k). This is so for the following reasons. The growth rate of employment (l) will in this case be less than the growth rate of the stock of machines; for if employment grew as much as the stock of machines, the marginal product of labour would fall because the supply of land had not also grown *pari passu* with the amounts of machinery and of employed labour. Of the three factors, therefore, land does not increase at all, labour in employment increases by an intermediate proportion, and the stock of machinery increases in the greatest proportion. Output, with constant returns to scale and with unchanged technical knowledge will, therefore, increase in a proportion less than that in which the stock of machines has increased; for it would have increased in the same proportion as the stock of machines only if land and labour had also increased by as high a proportion. But since $y < k$, $\dfrac{Y}{K}$ will be continually falling. With a constant S, therefore, $\dfrac{SY}{K}$ will be continually falling. The rate of capital accumulation will, therefore, be continually falling; and this in itself will tend to cause the rate of increase in the demand for labour continuously to fall.

Case (iii). Suppose next that while there are only two factors of production, land and machinery, there is continuous technical progress. Unless technical progress is so biassed in the direction of labour-saving as actually to lower the marginal product of a given amount of labour employed with a given amount of machinery, there will be a continuous tendency for the marginal product of labour to rise so long as the ratio of labour to machinery employed $\dfrac{L}{K}$ remains unchanged. At a constant real wage rate $\dfrac{L}{K}$ will therefore tend to rise. In other words l will now be greater than k. It follows that in this case y will be greater than k for two reasons: first, because labour is growing more rapidly than the only other factor machinery, output itself will be growing more rapidly than the stock of machinery; and, secondly, technical progress will itself be raising the amount of output produced by any given amount of the factors. But since $y > k$, $\dfrac{Y}{K}$ and, therefore, $\dfrac{SY}{K}$ will be rising. The rate of capital accumulation will be continuously rising; and this will tend to cause a continuous rise in the growth rate of the demand for labour.

We can say something more precise about these three cases, if we make the assumptions which in Chapter 4 resulted in a state of steady economic growth. Let us assume, that is to say, (i) that technical progress is neutral and (ii) that the elasticities of substitution between all the factors of production are equal to unity. As we have already seen (pages 30 to 33), in these conditions the proportions of the national income going to the three factors of production (Q, U, and Z) will all be constant.

Now when the proportion of the national income going to wages (Q) is constant, it follows that the growth rate of total wages will be the same as the growth rate of total national income; and with a constant real wage rate the growth rate in the volume of employment will be the same as the growth rate of total wages. In other words, we would now have

$$l = y.$$

We can now consider our basic relationship $y = Uk + Ql + r$, which still shows the rate at which production will grow (y) when the stock of machinery grows at a rate k and the amount of labour in employment at a rate l. But in our present case $l = y$, so that

$$y = \frac{U}{1-Q}k + \frac{r}{1-Q}$$
$$= \frac{U}{U+Z}k + \frac{r}{U+Z}.$$

By a process of reasoning exactly similar to that used in the last chapter (pages 35 to 39) we can see that the economy will now always tend towards a state of steady growth at which $y = k$. For suppose y to be greater than k. Then $\dfrac{Y}{K}$ is rising, so that $\dfrac{SY}{K}$ or k is rising. But this rise in k will cause y to rise by

$\dfrac{U}{U+Z}\ k$, i.e. by something less than k. This process of rises in k and lesser rises in y will continue until $y = k$. And similarly, if y were initially less than k, k would be falling; y would be falling by only $\dfrac{U}{U+Z}\ k$; and this would go on until $y = k$[1].

In other words with our present assumptions y will equal l, because the real wage rate is kept constant; and the economy will tend towards a steady state of growth with $y = k$. There will, therefore, be a state of steady growth in which $y = l = k$. If we set $y = k = l$ in the relationship $y = Uk + Ql + r$ we obtain

$$y = l = k = \frac{r}{Z}.$$

The economy will, therefore, with our present assumptions tend always to a state in which the growth rate in the demand for labour is equal to $\dfrac{r}{Z}$. If the demographic situation is such that the growth rate of the population is greater (or less) than $\dfrac{r}{Z}$, then in the state of steady growth the unemployment percentage will be continually rising (or falling).

If we consider the steady growth rate $\dfrac{r}{Z}$, it is clear that this is zero when r is zero. This is a special case of case (ii) discussed on pages 50 and 51 above. With our present assumption of elasticities of substitution equal to unity, the growth rate of the demand for labour will fall continuously towards zero if there is a third limiting factor land ($Z \neq 0$) but no technical progress. If there is any continuous growth of total population, sooner or later the unemployment percentage will start to rise.

Similarly, if we consider the case when there is no limiting third factor, land, ($Z = 0$), the steady growth rate $\dfrac{r}{Z}$ will rise to infinity;

---

[1] The reader can use Diagram II on page 37 to make clear the process, if he substitutes $\dfrac{r}{U+Z}$ for $r+Ql$ and $\dfrac{U}{U+Z}$ for U throughout the diagram and the text of Chapter 4.

this is a special case of case (iii) discussed on pages 51 and 52 above; with our present assumptions of neutral technical progress and of elasticities of substitution between the factors equal to unity, the growth rate in the demand for labour will grow without limit. However great the growth rate in the total population may be, sooner or later the unemployment percentage will tend to fall[1].

---

[1] If we consider the steady-state growth rate $\frac{r}{Z}$, when there is no third factor ($Z = 0$) and no technical progress ($r = 0$), we are in fact back at case (i) on pages 49 and 50 with a rate of steady growth equal to $\frac{SY_0}{K_0}$.

CHAPTER 6

An Alternative Treatment of Technical Progress

In the preceding chapters technical progress is defined as being neutral if, with unchanged supplies of all the factors, the marginal product of every factor is raised in the same proportion; this definition stems from that used by Professor Hicks in his *Theory of Wages*. An alternative definition has been very widely used recently by writers on the theory of economic growth according to which technical progress is neutral if the rate of profit remains constant when the ratio of the capital stock to national income remains constant; this type of definition stems from that used by Sir Roy Harrod in his *Towards a Dynamic Economics*. The present author would make two claims for the former type of treatment.

First, it provides a watertight definition even when there are a large number of factors of production. In the preceding chapters we have in fact used it when there were three factors of production, land, labour, and machinery. The latter definition, however, is imprecise when there are more than two factors of production. For whether or not the rate of profit remains constant when the capital stock increases at the same rate as total output will not be uniquely determined by what has happened to the state of technical knowledge; it may also be affected by what has happened to the ratio between the other factors of production—land and labour. This difficulty is non-existent if there are only two factors of production—labour and machinery—and there are constant returns to scale. For in that case the marginal product of machinery (i.e. the rate of profit) will depend solely upon what has happened to machinery per head and to technical knowledge, so that if machinery per head is assumed to have gone up in the same proportion as output per head, the result on the rate of profit will be uniquely determined by what has happened to technical knowledge.

Second, the use of the second of the two types of definition of neutral technical progress mentioned above almost inevitably involves a measurement 'of the rate of technical progress in terms of the growth rate of output which would occur not with a constant stock of real capital but either (i) with the capital stock growing at the same growth rate as output (so that the capital-output ratio is constant) or (ii) with the capital stock growing at a growth rate just sufficient to keep the rate of profit constant[1]. This seems to the present author an unnatural definition which ascribes to technical progress some element of the increase of output which is better ascribed to capital accumulation.

However, definitions are merely definitions; and the choice of one definition rather than of another is a matter mainly of convenience in use for the analysis of the real problem under examination. The purpose of this chapter is merely to explain the difference in the two types of definition and to explain some of the implications of this difference. The present author owes this to his readers since he has deliberately chosen a type of definition which is at present rather out of fashion with writers on the subject.

The basic implications of the two types of definitions are most easily examined on the assumption that there are only two factors, machinery and labour, and that the population is in fact constant. We are then considering only economic growth which is due either to the accumulation of capital and/or to improvements in technical knowledge. We can in this case use Diagram V on the next page, which is of the same kind as Diagram I (page 23) which we have already employed.

As we have already seen (pages 23 and 24) our definition of neutral technical progress involves a rise in the *slope* of the *F*-curve between A and B by the same proportion as the rise in the *height* of the *F*-curve between A and B. This means that, on an unchanged amount of capital, the marginal product of capital or the amount of profit per unit of capital will have gone up in the same proportion as total output; or in other words between A and B the proportion of total output which is paid out in profits remains constant if technical progress is neutral in our sense.

---

[1] This condition (ii) is the one made in the definitions used by D. G. Champernowne in his article on 'Capital Accumulation and the Maintenance of Full Employment' in the *Economic Journal*, June 1958. Condition (i) and condition (ii) come to the same thing if technical progress is assumed to be neutral in the alternative Harrodian sense which is under examination in this chapter.

Diagram V

In the alternative Harrodian sense technical progress is neutral if the slope of the F_2-curve at C is the same as the slope of the F_1-curve at A. For the straight line OAC, going through the origin O, gives the locus of all points at which the capital-output ratio $\left(\dfrac{K}{Y}\right)$ is constant at its initial value $\left(\dfrac{OD}{AD}\right)$; and by the Harrodian definition technical progress is neutral if the rate of profit or the marginal product of capital (i.e. the slope of the F-curve) remains unchanged when the capital-income ratio is unchanged. But if the rate of profit per unit of capital is unchanged and the ratio of capital to income is unchanged, then the ratio of total profits to national output is unchanged. In other words, the Harrodian type of definition involves an unchanged proportion of the national income going to profits between points A and C.

The two definitions come to exactly the same thing if the elasticity of substitution between labour and capital is equal to unity. For in this case as capital was accumulated and we moved along the F_2-curve from B to C, the distribution of income would be unchanged, because the fall in the rate of profit would just offset the rise in the amount of capital in its effect upon the distribution of income. But if the elasticity of substitution between labour and capital were greater than unity, then the movement from B to C would be associated with a rise in the proportion of the national income which went to profits, because the fall in the rate of profit between B and C would be less than sufficient to offset the effect of the increase in the amount of capital in increasing the proportion of the national income going to profits. If, therefore, technical progress were neutral in our (Hicksian) sense so that the proportion of income going to profits were unchanged between A and B, technical progress would be biassed in a capital-using direction in the alternative (Harrodian) usage, if the elasticity of substitution between capital and labour were greater than unity between B and C, since in this case the proportion of income going to profits would be raised between B and C and thus between A and C.

Let us turn to possible ways of defining the rate of technical progress when the alternative Harrodian type of definition of neutral technical progress is used. Mr Champernowne[1], for example, uses essentially the Harrodian definition of neutrality in technical progress and he measures the rate of technical progress as 'that growth rate of capital which would leave the rate of profit on capital unaffected, if population were stationary . . .'. Suppose for the moment that technical progress were neutral in the Harrodian sense so that in Diagram V the rate of profit at C would be the same as at A. Then Champernowne's measure of the rate of technical progress would be $\dfrac{DE}{OD}$ (i.e the proportionate increase in K needed to keep the rate of profit constant); but, in this case of neutral technical progress, $\dfrac{DE}{OD}$ by similar triangles equals $\dfrac{CH}{HE}$ or the proportionate increase in output which would occur from technical progress if simultaneously capital were accumulated to an extent sufficient to keep the capital-output ratio constant $\left(\dfrac{OE}{EC} = \dfrac{OD}{DA}\right)$. To define this as the rate of technical progress appears to the present author unnatural as the increment of output CH is partly due to improved technical knowledge (the rise

---

[1] *Loc. cit.*

in the F-curve) but partly also due to the accumulation of capital (DE) and the consequential movement to the right along the F-curve[1].

Suppose that we accept as the definition of the rate of technical progress the growth rate of output on the assumption that the capital-output ratio is kept constant (i.e. $\dfrac{\text{CH}}{\text{HE}}$ in Diagram V) instead of our definition of it as the growth rate of output on the assumption that the absolute amount of all factors, including the quantity of real capital, is kept constant (i.e. $\dfrac{\text{BA}}{\text{AD}}$ in Diagram V). It may be of interest to see how our previous measure can be expressed in terms of this new measure of the rate of technical progress.

Consider our basic growth relationship $y = Uk + Ql + r$, when the population is constant (i.e. $l = 0$). Then we have

$$y = Uk + r.$$

Now the new measure of the rate of technical progress (which we will write as $\bar{r}$) is the growth rate in output when population is constant and when the growth rate of capital is the same as the growth rate of output ($y = k$) so that the capital-output ratio is kept constant. Now when $y = k$, we have $y = Uy + r$ or $y = \dfrac{r}{1 - U}$. But in this case $y = \bar{r}$, so that

$$\bar{r} = \frac{r}{1 - U}.$$

---

[1] The precise definition used by Champernowne becomes even more unnatural if technical progress is very biassed in the direction of being very capital-saving or capital-using (in the Harrodian sense which Champernowne is himself using). Suppose that technical progress were very capital-saving in this sense and that the slope of the F_2-curve at B were the same as the slope of the old curve at A. Then by Champernowne's definition the rate of technical progress would be zero, since no growth of capital is required to keep the marginal product of capital constant. Indeed, if the rate of technical progress were so capital-saving that the point of equal slope on the F_2-curve lay to the left of B, as at J in Diagram V, we should have to measure the rate of technical progress as a negative quantity, namely $-\dfrac{\text{LD}}{\text{OD}}$. Champernowne's measure of the rate of technical progress is thus a mixture of the amount of innovation and of the capital-saving or capital-using nature of that innovation.

We will call r 'our' definition of the rate of technical progress and $\bar{r}$ the 'alternative' definition of the rate of technical progress, i.e. the growth rate of output per head due to technical progress if real capital stock per unit of output is kept constant.

Let us apply the 'alternative' definition to the problem examined in the last chapter and on the assumption of only two factors of production. Conditions (i) and (ii) on page 30 now boil down to the single condition that technical progress is neutral in the 'alternative' sense examined in this section; for, as we have seen, if technical progress is neutral in 'our' sense and if the elasticity of substitution between labour and capital is equal to unity, technical progress will also be neutral in the 'alternative' sense.

As we showed in the last chapter, in these conditions the growth rate of the capital stock (k) and the growth rate of output (y) will both tend towards the steady growth rate of $\dfrac{Ql+r}{1-U}$. Now in the conditions in which there are constant returns to scale and only two factors of production $Q = 1 - U$ (see page 16 above). Moreover, if we use the 'alternative' measure of the rate of technical progress we can write $\dfrac{r}{1-U} = \bar{r}$. We can thus say that in these conditions the growth rates of the capital stock and of output will both tend towards the steady growth rate of $l + \bar{r}$. This is, indeed, Mrs Robinson's Golden Age, where output and capital stock both grow at the same steady rate which is equal to the sum of the growth rate of population (l) and the growth rate of output per head ($\bar{r}$).

CHAPTER 7

The Rigidity of Machinery

Up to this point we have been working on the assumption of perfect malleability of machinery. That is to say, we have assumed that our capital good (e.g. steel) can be made into machines of different forms to suit the current state of technical knowledge and to suit the ratios of labour and land to machinery which the current costs of the different factors makes profitable; we have also assumed that the tonnage of steel incorporated in any machine can in the short run as well as in the long run be readily and without cost transformed into a different type of machine which is more profitable in the light of changing technical knowledge and of changing relative scarcities of the factors of production. This assumption has enabled us to work with a production function in which at any one moment of time the normal rate of output is uniquely determined by the amount of the three factors available for production—acres of land, man-hours of labour, and the tonnage of steel incorporated in the existing stock of machinery, this machinery always being present in its most useful form; and this production function has allowed a continuous variation in the proportions between the various factors.

The assumption of perfect malleability of machinery is, of course, an unrealistic one. It obscures some important problems of economic growth. The fact that particular machines are in fact constructed to be operated by a more or less rigidly fixed number of operatives or to produce a more or less rigidly fixed rate of output of the final product introduces a major problem in economic growth. How in fact is equilibrium growth now to be achieved, when it is essential for equilibrium that the number *and form* of machines should be such as to match changes in the amount of the other factors (e.g. working population) and in technical knowledge?

Let us for the moment examine this problem on a set of assumptions which is the exact reverse of that of the perfect malleability of machinery. Let us suppose that both in the long run and in the short run there is perfect rigidity in the form of machinery in the sense that a given tonnage of steel can be made only into one type of machine which for technical reasons must be used either (i) to produce a given rate of output or (ii) to be operated with a given amount of labour. In case (i) one ton of steel can be made only into one loom of a kind which will produce a fixed amount of cloth per hour; and in this case increased productivity due to technical progress would show itself in a reduction in the amount of labour needed to tend a loom. In case (ii) one ton of steel can be made only into one loom of a kind which must be operated by one worker; and in this case increased productivity due to technical progress would show itself in an increase in the amount of cloth produced by the one-man-one-loom team. We will examine these two cases in turn[1].

Case (i). Suppose the population to be growing at a rate l and suppose that output per head is growing, as a result of technical progress, at a rate $\bar{r}$. Then total output must grow at a rate equal to $l + \bar{r}$ in order to give full employment, but not more than full employment, to the labour force. We may call this growth rate the 'natural rate of growth' (following Sir Roy Harrod's usage). Since we are assuming that the amount of real capital required per unit of output is rigidly fixed for technical reasons, the amount of machinery would have to rise at this same rate, $l + \bar{r}$, in order that the supply of machinery should match the supply of labour. But the stock of machinery will in fact rise at a rate equal to $\dfrac{SY}{K}$

since people will be saving an amount of income equal to SY and the investment of these savings in new machinery will cause the stock of machines to increase by an amount equal to SY or by a proportion equal to $\dfrac{SY}{K}$. But since we are assuming that a fixed output can be produced by each unit of machinery, output must

---

[1] It should be borne in mind that in this chapter we are not yet modifying the assumption of the perfect substitutability in production between consumption goods and capital goods. That is to say, we still assume that, however rigidly the ratio between them may be fixed, nevertheless any combination of labour and machinery which will produce one unit of consumption goods will also serve to produce one unit of capital goods.

also be rising at a rate equal to $\dfrac{SY}{K}$ in order to give full employment, but not more than full employment, to the available supply of machinery. We may call this the 'warranted rate of growth'.

Case (ii). Suppose population to be growing at the rate l and output per head to be growing at the rate r. Then output must grow at a rate equal to $l+r$ in order to give full employment, but not more than full employment, to the labour force. We may now call this the 'natural rate of growth'. But, as before, the capital stock will rise at a rate equal to $\dfrac{SY}{K}$ and, in this case, output per machine will be rising at the rate r; for in this case the ratio of machinery to labour is rigidly fixed and the growth rate in product per machine will be the same as the growth rate in product per man (r). The growth rate in output which is necessary to give full employment, but not more than full employment, to the increasing supply of machinery will thus be $\dfrac{SY}{K}+r$, which will represent the 'warranted rate of growth' in this case.

Now if the warranted rate of growth is less than the natural rate of growth ($\dfrac{SY}{K} < l+\bar{r}$ in case (i) or $\dfrac{SY}{K} < l$ in case (ii)) there will be a tendency for the stock of machinery to accumulate at a rate which is less rapid than is necessary to fit in with the growth of the labour force. There will be a growing shortage of machinery and a growing over-abundance of labour, some of which must remain idle in 'technological' or 'disguised' unemployment because of a lack of machinery for it to work with. In the opposite case where the warranted rate of growth is greater than the natural rate of growth ($\dfrac{SY}{K} > l+\bar{r}$ in case (i) or $\dfrac{SY}{K} > l$ in case (ii)), there will be a tendency for the stock of machinery to grow more quickly than is required to match the labour force, so that some machines will tend to lie idle for lack of workers to operate them[1].

---

[1] In this latter case, it will, of course, be very difficult to prevent a general slump in economic activity; for it will be difficult with existing machinery idle or used below capacity to maintain the incentives to invest in new additional

(footnote continued on page 64

In these conditions there remains one mechanism in the economic system which might bring the natural and the warranted rates of growth into line with each other even though there were a technically rigidly fixed ratio between the amount of machinery and the level of output (case (i)) or between the amount of machinery and the amount of labour in employment (case (ii)). An equilibrating mechanism might work through the effects of the relative supplies of labour and of machinery upon the distribution of the national income between profits and wages, and thus upon the proportion of the national income which is saved, and thus upon the warranted rate of growth itself. Let us explain this possibility in rather more detail.

Where there are rigid ratios of the kind which we have been examining between machinery and output or between machinery and men, the marginal products of machinery and men lose their meaning. This is most easily seen in case (ii) above, where the amount of machinery in use per worker is rigidly fixed. In this case if there is any excess supply of labour, the marginal product of labour is zero, since nothing can be added to output by having one more worker without any change in the amount of the other factors. But if there is any excess of machinery, then the marginal product of labour becomes equal to the total output which would be produced by having one more worker and one more machine in employment, since the additional worker would enable an idle machine to be brought into use. If, however, the supplies of machinery and labour were initially exactly matched, the marginal product of labour would be indeterminate between these two extremes; nothing could be added to output by one more worker without any change in the amount of machinery available for

---

(footnote continued from page 63

machinery on a scale necessary to make use of all the savings (SY) forthcoming from the national income if it is maintained at its full employment level. The economy will thus be prone to lapse into a stagnant state in which neither machinery nor men are fully employed. Since, however, it is our purpose in this book to examine only the problems of growth in an economy in which general booms and slumps are avoided, we must assume that the government takes steps to avoid such stagnation in the economy. For example, the government may have a public-works policy whereby it borrows the excess savings to spend on the excess supply of machines in order to hold them off the private market. The remainder of the output of new machines would no longer be in excess of the amount needed to match the growing labour force.

employment, while the loss of one worker would cause the loss of the output of one-worker-plus-one-machine.

Similarly, in case (i) where the amount of machinery per unit of output was rigidly fixed, the marginal product of labour alone would be indeterminate between zero (if there was no idle machinery available to go with the additional output of an additional worker) and the output due to having one more worker plus the additional machinery necessary to go with the worker's additional output. In either case the distribution of income between profits and wages in a competitive economy could no longer be determined by the proportional marginal products of the two factors (U and Q), as we have hitherto assumed to be so. These concepts are meaningful only where it is possible at the margin to vary the ratio of machinery to labour in accordance with the relative prices of the two factors, substituting the one which was cheap relatively to the value of its marginal product for the one which was relatively expensive.

In a competitive economy in which there are rigidly fixed ratios between machinery and output or between machinery and labour, an excess supply of the one factor and a deficient supply of the other might be expected, nevertheless, to cause the earnings of the former to fall and of the latter to rise. Suppose, for example, that the natural rate of growth were above the warranted rate of growth; that, in consequence, the available supply of labour tended to outstrip the available supply of machinery; and that some labour was in consequence idle while all the machinery was fully occupied. In such circumstances (assuming always, as we are, that the authorities adopted some financial policy which ensured an unlimited market for consumption goods at a stable selling price) entrepreneurs would compete with each other to take on more machinery and workers would compete with each other to sell more labour. The profit per machine that would be offered to attract more machines would rise[1], and the wage that had to be paid per worker would fall. As profits rose and wages fell, the proportion of the national income that was saved would rise if the propensity to save out of profits were greater than the

---

[1] As the rate of profit rose the monetary authorities might have to raise the rate of interest at which money could be borrowed to prevent such a growth in the incentive to borrow money to invest in new machinery as to cause a general inflation in demand and so in the price of consumption goods.

propensity to save out of wages. The rate at which machinery could be accumulated without any general inflationary pressures being set up would be raised; and by this process the warranted rate of growth would be raised towards the natural rate of growth. It is possible that after a sufficient change in the distribution of income due to the rise in the rate of profit and the fall in the rate of wages savings would be so stimulated that the growth rate in the stock of machinery could be raised to correspond to the growth rate in the labour force.

In the opposite circumstances, where the growth rate in the stock of capital was initially too high to match the growth rate in the labour force there would develop a shortage of labour and a superfluity of machines; competition would drive down the profit per machine and drive up the wage per worker in conditions in which financial policy was such as to maintain an unlimited market for the sale of finished consumption goods at a stable selling price[1]; the consequential shift of income from profits to wages would reduce the proportion of the national income which was saved in so far as wage-earners had a lower propensity to save than profit-makers; and in consequence the growth rate in the stock of machinery would be reduced more nearly into line with the growth of the labour force.

A given change in the distribution of income between wages and profits would do more to close any gap between the two growth rates, the greater were the divergence between the propensities to save out of profits and wages. But this mechanism would suffice to restore equilibrium only if the proportion of profits saved were above the level of S which was necessary to make the warranted rate of growth equal to the natural rate of growth and if at the same time the proportion of wages saved were below the level of S required to equate the warranted and the natural rates of growth. Suppose, for example, that the proportion of profits saved as well as the proportion of wages saved was below the level of S which was required to give the growth rate in the stock of machinery

---

[1] As we have seen (footnote on page 63) such a policy might involve the authorities in taking excess machinery off the market through a 'public-works' policy. In this case we must envisage the authorities at the same time bidding up the wage rate by trying to hire labour to man-up their idle machines and lowering the profit per machine by offering to hire out their idle machines cheaply to private enterprise.

which matched the growth rate in the labour force. Then the labour force would tend to get too big for the stock of machinery; even if by the process described above this caused wages to fall to zero so that the whole of the national income went to profits, savings, though higher than before, would still be too small to allow the stock of machinery to grow in line with the labour force. And conversely, if the proportion of wages saved as well as the proportion of profits saved was above the level necessary to keep the growth rate of machinery in line with the growth rate of the labour force, then, even if the relative oversupply of machinery and scarcity of labour reduced profits to zero and raised wages to absorb the whole national income, the rate of accumulation of machinery (which would be necessary to absorb in investment all the savings of the wage-earners) would still be higher than was required to match the growth rate of the labour force. This mechanism of equilibrium through the distribution of income would, however, be very effective if the proportion of profits saved lay well above, and the proportion of wages saved lay well below, the critical value of S (i.e. $\frac{K}{Y}(l+\bar{r})$ in case (i) on page 62 and $\frac{K}{Y}l$ in case (ii) on page 63)[1].

But in making the assumption that there is complete rigidity in the ratio of machinery to output or of machinery to men we have gone much too far in the other direction. In fact there is very considerable possibility of adjustment in these ratios in four different ways. Let us illustrate these by supposing that the money wage rate rises, while—because of financial policy—the selling price of finished products remains constant. This rise in the wage rate we will suppose to occur because of a scarcity of labour relative to machinery. Our question is to ask how this rise in the cost of labour may cause entrepreneurs to use a lower ratio of labour to machinery and thus to restore a balance between the available machinery and the available labour force.

There are two ways in which there may be an immediate short-run effect upon the ratio of machinery to men.

---

[1] The observant reader will notice a strong family relationship between the analysis in the above paragraphs and Mr Kaldor's theory of distribution. See his article 'Alternative Theories of Distribution' in the *Review of Economic Studies*, March 1956.

In the first place, while existing machinery may be designed to be operated with a given amount of labour or to produce a given rate of output, there are some possibilities even in the short run of varying output at the margin by taking on more or less men with a given equipment of plant and machinery. A rise in the wage rate may cause some of the efforts to squeeze the most out of a given equipment to be relaxed; less intensive operation may now be profitable.

But, secondly, a rise in the wage rate may make the most ancient and obsolete forms of machinery unprofitable so that they are scrapped rather sooner than would otherwise be the case. A machine, once it exists, will tend to be operated so long as any profit over and above the prime costs of production can be realised on its operation. A rise in the wage rate will represent a rise in prime costs; the result may be to turn a profit into a loss on working the most obsolete forms of machinery. If these old machines are scrapped more quickly, more labour is released to be employed with the newly accumulated up-to-date machines.

Thus even in the short run a rise in the real wage rate may serve to adjust an excess stock of machinery to a deficient labour force by making it profitable to employ rather less men with existing machines or to scrap some existing machines entirely, before they would otherwise have been scrapped. But it is in its longer-run effect upon the form in which new machinery will be installed that a rise in the real wage rate may have its most marked effect upon the ratio of machinery to men; and this longer-run effect may also operate in two ways.

In the first place, the more expensive is the hire of labour and the less expensive is the hire of a machine the less labour-intensive and the more machine-intensive will be the most profitable techniques of production. With cheap labour it may be profitable to use a ton of steel to produce a large number of cheap looms, each to be operated by a separate worker; but with expensive labour it may be more profitable to use the ton of steel to produce one single elaborate automatic loom which will require only one worker to operate it. The more expensive labour becomes and the more expensive it is expected to become, the higher the ratio of machinery to men appropriate to the forms of machinery which will be newly installed. And these newly installed machines with this high machine-labour ratio will be installed both out of depreciation allowances to replace old machines as they wear out or are scrapped and also out of net new savings to add to the existing stock of machinery.

But, secondly, our assumption that there is only one consumption good hides another important possibility. In fact consumption goods are of many kinds and vary greatly in their requirements of men and machinery for their production; they range from pure services which require almost wholly men for their provision to certain products which require elaborate and expensive machinery and very little labour for their making. A rise in the cost of hiring labour and a fall in the cost of hiring machinery will raise the cost-price of consumption services whose costs depend almost solely upon the wages of the 'servants' concerned and will lower the cost-price of consumption goods of a very machinery-intensive nature in their production. As a result the demand for the latter type of consumption goods will expand relatively to the demand for the former type of consumption service. New machinery (financed both out of depreciation allowances and out of new savings) will tend to go more and more into the production of those products which require a high ratio of machinery to men in their making.

To summarise. One of the main problems of maintaining equilibrium in economic growth is to keep the amount and the form of the supply of machinery in line with the total labour force which must be employed with it. If, for example, the growth rate of the stock of machinery tends to outstrip the growth rate of the labour force, then (assuming always a successful adoption of a financial policy by the authorities which provides an unlimited market for final consumption goods at a stable price level for such goods) the competitive process will tend to raise the wage per worker and to lower the profit per machine. This change in factor prices will help in five ways to restore a balance between the supplies of machinery and the labour force:

(i) It will make it profitable to use existing equipment somewhat less intensively.

(ii) It will make it profitable to scrap some existing equipment more quickly than would otherwise be the case.

(iii) It will make it profitable to use depreciation allowances and new savings to construct new machinery for the production of any given product by techniques which involve a higher ratio of machinery to labour.

(iv) It will make it profitable to use depreciation allowances and new savings for the construction of machinery in those industries which produce consumption goods which require a high ratio of machinery to labour in their production. And

(v) if, in spite of (i) to (iv), there is not much rapid substitution of machinery for labour it will cause a fall in total profits and a rise in total wages and this shift of income from profits to wages may cause a reduction in the proportion of the national income which is saved, which will reduce the equilibrium growth rate of the capital stock and bring it more in line with the growth rate of the labour force.

It is by the joint operation of these five forces, against the background of a stabilising financial policy, that in the real world machines and men may be kept in balance.

CHAPTER 8

The Price of Capital Goods

Let us now modify the assumption of 'perfect substitutability in production between capital goods and consumption goods' (cf. page 6 above). By this we have implied (i) that the rate and nature of technical progress in the two industries is the same, (ii) that the factor-intensities of production in the two industries are the same, and (iii) that machines are perfectly malleable in the sense that the amount of the capital good (e.g. steel) embodied in a machine which was producing capital goods could instantaneously and without cost be transformed into a machine suitable for producing consumption goods.

In such conditions the cost-price of a capital good in terms of a consumption good would always remain constant. Assumption (i) above would mean that the costs of capital goods were not moving differently from those of consumption goods as a result of technical progress. Assumption (ii) means that if the relative prices of the factors alter (if, for example, the real wage-rate rises and the profit per machine falls because of capital accumulation) this will not affect the cost of capital goods differently from the cost of consumption goods, because both products have the same mix of factor prices in their make-up of costs.

Without assumption (iii) movements in the price of capital goods might differ from movements in the price of consumption goods because of unexpected shifts of demand between the two products, leading to a divergence of short-run prices from long-run costs. Suppose, for example, that producers had made an error of forecast and had anticipated in the case of the production of capital goods a higher level of demand than materialised and in the case of consumption goods a lower level of demand than materialised. Then their investment programmes would have led to a temporary shortage of machinery in the capital-goods industries and to a temporary superfluity of machinery in the consumption-goods industries. Prices and quasi-rents on machinery would be temporarily high in the case of capital-goods output relatively to prices and quasi-rents in the consumption-goods industries. But this would not be the case if machinery were perfectly malleable so that the superfluous machinery in the consumption-goods industries could be used to fill the gap in the capital-goods industries or if—what comes to much the same thing—there were perfect foresight on the part of producers so that machinery always existed at any one time in its most useful form.

But even if we continue, in accordance with assumption (iii), to consider only the case of equilibrium growth in which such temporary disequilibria do not occur, there remain some important reasons why the equilibrium price of capital goods may be rising or falling in terms of consumption goods[1].

First, the price of capital goods may be rising because of the nature of technical progress which may be tending to reduce the real cost of consumption goods more rapidly than that of capital goods. It is to be noted that there are now two quite separate forms of bias in the nature of technical progress. Suppose for simplification that there were only two factors, labour and machinery, and that the factor-intensities of the two industries were the same. Then one might have a case in which the rate of rise (resulting from technical progress) of the marginal product of labour in the consumption-goods industry was the same as that of the marginal product of machinery in the consumption-goods industry and that the rate of rise of the marginal product of labour in the capital-goods industry was the same as that of the marginal product of machinery in the capital-goods industry; then technical progress would be neither labour-saving nor labour-using as we have defined those terms (see pages 19 to 21 above); but if the growth rate (due to technical progress) of the marginal products of both labour and of machinery were lower in the capital-goods industries than in the consumption-goods industries, technical progress

---

[1] The remaining paragraphs of this chapter deal only in a rather cursory manner with one of the issues raised by the possibility that the price of capital goods may vary relatively to the price of consumption goods. We are in fact now dealing with a fairly complex set of relationships between many variables. Appendix II is devoted to a more profound discussion of these relationships. In that Appendix all the main issues which we have discussed in Chapters 1 to 7 in the case of a one-product economy are applied (alas! in mathematical terms) to an economy producing two products, a capital good and a quite distinct consumption good.

(though neither labour-saving nor labour-using nor machinery-saving nor machinery-using) would be biassed in such a way as to raise the cost-price of capital goods relatively to that of consumption goods. We may call this a bias against capital goods. Or, to take the other extreme case, the growth rate (due to technical progress) of the marginal product of labour might be the same in both industries and that of the marginal product of machinery might be the same in both industries; there would be no bias in technical progress tending to raise or to lower the cost of capital goods in terms of consumption goods; but if the growth rate in the marginal product of labour were in both industries higher than the growth rate in the marginal product of machinery, there would nevertheless be a labour-using and machinery-saving bias in technical progress[1].

Second, if the factor-intensities of the two industries producing capital goods and consumption goods differ, then anything which causes the relative price of the factors of production to change over time will cause the cost price of capital goods to change relatively to the cost price of consumption goods. If, for example, the production of capital goods involved the use of a lot of labour and of little machinery whereas the production of consumption goods involved the use of little labour but much machinery[2], then a rise in the wage per worker relatively to the profit per machine would raise the cost-price of capital goods relatively to that of consumption goods.

Now there are two quite separate reasons why relative factor prices may alter in this way, the one cause operating through the relative demand for the two products and so for the factors and the other operating through the relative supply of the factors.

---

[1] See Appendix II, Section (2), pages 134 and 135 for a further discussion of this point.

[2] An extreme form of this pattern would be one where the earlier stages of production (the capital-good industry) use only primary factors of production (land and labour) in order to produce instruments of production (machines) which are used only in the later stages of production (the consumption-good industry) to produce the final product (consumption goods). But there is no reason why this should be the predominant pattern. The capital-goods industries might well be more machine-intensive than the consumption-goods industries. The only thing which would be ridiculous would be that the consumption-goods industries should employ no machinery; for the production of machines useful only to produce more machines would be absurd.

Let us first consider the demand side. Suppose that for some reason (for example, because rising real income and standards of living cause a larger and larger proportion of the national income to be saved) the amount spent on capital goods rises relatively to the amount spent on consumption goods. This relative shift of demand away from consumption goods onto capital goods will indirectly represent a relative shift away from the factors of production needed to produce consumption goods onto the factors of production needed to produce capital goods. Suppose, as before, that capital goods are labour-intensive and consumption goods machine-intensive in their production; then the shift of demand from consumption goods onto capital goods will tend to raise the wage per worker relatively to the profit per machine, and this will tend to raise the cost-price of labour-intensive capital goods relatively to the cost-price of machinery-intensive consumption goods[1].

But suppose next that the proportion of the national income saved (and so the ratio of expenditure on capital goods to expenditure on consumption goods) remained constant. The profit per machine might nevertheless fall relatively to the wage per worker because of a change in the supplies of the factors. Suppose that the proportion of income saved is high so that in equilibrium growth there is a high growth rate in the stock of machinery, and suppose that the population is growing only slowly. Then the amount of machinery to be employed per head will be growing; and for it to be profitable for entrepreneurs to change their techniques so as to employ a higher ratio of machinery per head, the profit per machine must fall relatively to the wage per worker. But this in turn will raise the cost price of capital goods in terms of consumption goods if capital goods are labour-intensive and consumption goods are machine-intensive in production; and it will

---

[1] This is, of course, merely an example of the familiar proposition of increasing costs due to differing factor proportions. It is to be observed that in the case discussed in the text we should have the same result (namely, a shift of demand from consumption goods into capital goods causing a rise in the cost price of capital goods in terms of consumption goods) if the capital goods had been machine-intensive and the consumption goods labour-intensive. But in this case the shift of demand would have tended to raise the profit per machine (which would have raised the cost of machinery-intensive capital goods) and to have lowered the wage per worker (which would have reduced the cost of labour-intensive consumption-goods).

lower the cost-price of capital goods if capital goods are machine-intensive and consumption goods are labour-intensive in production.

The problem discussed in the preceding paragraph lies at the centre of the basic problem of economic growth discussed in the last chapter. To maintain a growing economy in equilibrium involves some mechanism which keeps the demand for the various factors in line with each other as they grow at differing rates. Let us continue to illustrate the problem by assuming that the stock of machinery has a higher growth rate than the working population, and let us simplify our discussion of the problem now at issue by supposing that there are no changes in technical knowledge taking place and no shifts in demand between capital goods and consumption goods (i.e. no change in the proportions of the national income spent on consumption goods and saved for expenditure on newly produced capital goods). The growing ratio of the supply of machines available for use per head will mean that equilibrium can be maintained only if the wage per worker rises relatively to the profit per machine sufficiently to induce entrepreneurs to use more machine-intensive techniques of production to the necessary extent. The speed with which the wage per worker must rise relatively to the profit per machine will depend essentially upon two sets of factors: (i) the higher the growth rate in the stock of machinery and the lower the growth rate of the population, the more rapidly must entrepreneurs be raising the ratio of machinery to labour in their production techniques; and (ii) the smaller the elasticity of substitution between labour and machinery, the more rapidly must the wage rate be rising relatively to the profit per machine to bring about any given rate of increase in the ratio of machinery to labour in employment. We have discussed these issues in earlier chapters of this book. We do not intend to repeat that discussion here. Let us assume then, by way of numerical illustration, that the growth in the supply of machinery is such, given the technical possibilities of substitution between machinery and labour, that a rise in the wage per worker relatively to the profit per machine of 10 per cent per annum is required to induce entrepreneurs to change their techniques at the necessary rate.

What we wish to discuss here are the problems raised by the various ways in which the necessary 10 per cent rise in the wage per worker relatively to the profit per machine might be occurring. We will take the four possible cases shown in Table I to illustrate the various possibilities. The fundamental point is that the profit per machine (row d) may change for either of two reasons: either

Table I.—*Growth Rates in the Cost of Using Labour Relatively to the Cost of Using Machinery* (*Growth Rates in Percentages Per Annum*)

		Cases:			
		I	II	III	IV
Growth rate in wage rate	(a)	+8	+2	+2	+2
Growth rate in rate of profit	(b)	−2	−8	−5	−11
Growth rate in price of machines	(c)	0	0	−3	+3
Growth rate in profit per machine = (b)+(c)	(d)	−2	−8	−8	−8
Growth rate in the cost of using labour relatively to the cost of using machinery = (a)−(d)	(e)	10	10	10	10

because of a change in the rate of profit (row b) or because of a change in the price of a machine (row c). Thus it may become cheaper to employ a machine either because the rate of profit which it is necessary to earn on any given capital sum has fallen (the price of a machine remaining unchanged) or because the price of a machine has fallen (the rate of profit on any given capital sum remaining unchanged). The complication of our present problem is due to the fact that the change in the cost price of a machine will itself depend upon what has happened to the profit per machine relatively to the wage per worker and upon the factor intensities of making capital goods (for use as machines) relatively to those of making consumption goods.

In Cases I and II in Table I we assume that the factor-intensities in the two industries producing capital goods and consumption goods are the same. This will mean that the cost price of capital goods remains unchanged in terms of consumption goods. But the rise of 10 per cent in the wage per worker relatively to the profit per machine (which we assume to be necessary to maintain equilibrium) can still be brought about in either of two ways: either by a large rise in the wage per worker combined with a small fall in the profit per machine (Case I) or else by a small rise in the wage per worker combined with a large fall in the profit per machine (Case II). Now Case I will apply in an economy in which a large proportion of the national income goes to profits and only a small proportion to wages. For in such a case a large percentage rise in the wage per worker will absorb only a moderate absolute amount of income, while a small percentage fall in the profit per machine will suffice to release the same absolute amount of income. It can thus be seen that in order to achieve a 10 per cent rise in the wage per worker relatively to the profit per machine, the wage per worker must rise by a large proportion and the profit per machine must fall by a small proportion if the economy is one in which a large proportion of the national income goes to profits and only a small proportion to wages (Case I). Conversely, if a large proportion of the national income goes to wages and only a small proportion to profits, a 10 per cent rise in the wage per worker relatively to the profit per machine must be brought about by a small percentage rise of the wage per worker and a large percentage fall of the profit per machine[1].

In Cases III and IV we continue the assumption made in Case II that a small proportion of the total national income is paid in profits and a large proportion in wages, so that in all these three cases, of the necessary 10 per cent rise in the wage of labour relatively to the profit per machine, only 2 per cent takes the form of a rise in the wage per worker and the remaining 8 per cent takes the form of a fall in the profit per machine. But the rate of profit will not necessarily fall by 8 per cent. It will do so if the cost price of a machine does not change (Case II); but if the cost price of a machine fell, then the rate of profit need fall so much the less in order to produce the necessary 8 per cent fall in the profit per machine (Case III); on the other hand, if the cost price

---

[1] See Appendix II, Section (2), pages 142 to 146.

of a machine rose, then the rate of profit would have to fall so much the more in order to produce an 8 per cent fall in the profit per machine.

Now with a 10 per cent rise in the cost of using a unit of labour relative to the cost of using a unit of machinery (all Cases), the cost price of producing capital goods relatively to the cost price of producing consumption goods will stay the same if there is no difference in the factor intensities in the two industries (Cases I and II), will fall if capital goods are more machine-intensive than consumption goods (Case III), and will rise if capital goods are more labour-intensive than consumption goods (Case IV).

We may conclude, therefore, that the more labour-intensive and the less machine-intensive is the production of capital goods relatively to the production of consumption goods, the more rapidly will the cost price of new machines rise and the more necessary it will be to rely on a fall in the rate of profit to achieve any given fall in profit per machine[1].

---

[1] With our assumptions of depreciation by evaporation and of the perfect malleability of machines the prevailing net profit per machine is the right measure of the opportunity cost of using a machine for the entrepreneur to compare with the wage of a worker in choosing his technique of production. But for the control of total investment the monetary authorities must keep the rate of interest at which money capital can be borrowed in line with the rate of profit (as we have defined it) plus the rate of rise in the price of a machine; for the total gain from an investment in an additional machine is the net profit earned by it plus any appreciation in its capital value. (Cf. Appendix II page 154.) In other words if, for example, the rate of profit were 6 per cent per annum, the rate of interest would have to be about 6 per cent per annum in Cases I and II, about 3 per cent per annum in Case III, and about 9 per cent per annum in Case IV. In all four Cases, however, the rate of interest would have to be changing so as to keep in line with the sum of the fall in the rate of profit plus any decline in (or minus any increase in) the rate of rise of machine prices.

CHAPTER 9

Depreciation and Replacement[1]

Let us restore the assumption that the cost price of a new machine is constant; but let us drop the assumption of depreciation by evaporation, namely that, whatever the date at which different component parts of the stock of machines were built in the past, a certain fixed proportion of that stock (say 10 per cent) falls to bits and needs to be replaced each year. Let us substitute for this assumption the assumption that every machine lasts for a given number of years (say, 10 years) with undiminished productivity and unchanged running costs, but then collapses. Machines thus die of sudden old age, and we will call this the principle of depreciation by sudden death.

Now in the case of depreciation by evaporation there can be no divergence between the depreciation allowance that should be deducted from gross profits to maintain the value of the machinery and the replacement expenditure which must be made to maintain the physical volume of machinery in existence. If 10 per cent of the existing stock of machinery collapses each year regardless of the age of the machinery (depreciation by evaporation), then it is exactly as if the machinery lasted for ever provided that an amount was spent each year on its repair and maintenance equal to 10 per cent of the value of the capital stock. In every year a depreciation allowance must be made equal to 10 per cent of the value of the capital stock and this same sum must be spent on new machinery in order to maintain the stock.

---

[1] Much of the substance of this chapter and of the accompanying Appendix III is due to the note by D. G. Champernowne and R. F. Kahn on 'The Value of Invested Capital' (reproduced at the end of Mrs Robinson's book on *The Accumulation of Capital*) and to the article by Professor E. D. Domar on 'Depreciation, Replacement, and Growth' (reprinted in his *Essays in the Theory of Economic Growth*). This chapter was already written before I saw Mrs Robinson's article entitled 'Depreciation' (published in the *Revista di Politica Economica* for November 1959) in which many of the relationships discussed in this chapter are also demonstrated.

But with depreciation by sudden death this is by no means the case. Let us suppose that a machine costs £1,000 to install, brings in a gross profit of £200 in each of the following 10 years, and collapses on the tenth anniversary of its instalment[1]. Then no replacement expenditure at all will be required until the tenth year after its installation when £1,000 must be spent on its replacement. A fund worth £1,000 must be built up by annual deductions from the gross profits earned by the machine over the ten years of its life. During these ten years annual depreciation allowances will be made, but no replacement expenditure will be incurred; in the tenth year of its productive life a replacement expenditure of £1,000 will be made, a sum which will be much in excess of any depreciation allowance made in that year.

If the owner of our machine wishes to maintain the value of his capital intact he must deduct something each year from his current annual receipts for a depreciation allowance in order to build up a fund by the tenth year equal to £1,000, the initial value of the machine, in order to purchase a new machine to replace the old machine. We shall call this deduction from the year's current receipts the depreciation allowance; but before we proceed it is necessary to clear up one possible source of confusion. As the machine ages, so the total depreciation fund will grow with each year's depreciation allowance added to it; the machine will become less and less valuable but the depreciation fund will become bigger and bigger; the money available in the growing depreciation fund can be invested in securities and will itself earn interest at 15 per cent per annum, the current rate of interest, so that as the machine ages there will be a larger and larger receipt of interest each year on the securities accumulated in the depreciation fund in readiness for the purchase of a new machine in the tenth year. There is a possible source of simple confusion in the treatment of the interest earned on the depreciation fund.

---

[1] In this case the net rate of interest earned on the machine would be 15 per cent per annum. The present value of £200 for 10 years at a rate of interest of 15 per cent per annum is $\frac{£200}{0\cdot15}\left(1-\frac{1}{1\cdot15^{10}}\right)$—see Appendix III, page 173—and this is equal to £1,000. In this chapter our numerical examples will, unless otherwise stated, be all based on the assumption that a new machine costs £1,000 and also has an initial market value of £1,000 because it will produce a gross profit of £200 for each of the following 10 years in a world in which the rate of interest is constant at 15 per cent per annum.

DEPRECIATION AND REPLACEMENT

Let us illustrate this by our numerical example. Consider again our machine which will earn £200 a year profit for each of ten years in an economy in which the rate of interest is 15 per cent and the cost of a new machine is £1,000. Suppose we have reached a point in the history of the machine in which £500 has been accumulated in the depreciation fund for the machine. Then the firm in that year will have a gross profit on its operations of £200 and interest on the depreciation fund of £75, a total current revenue of £275. Suppose that this year it adds another £100 to the depreciation fund, raising it from £500 to £600. Then there are two ways in which these figures might be laid out in its accounts:

Method I

A. Trading Profits

Profits available for Distribution £175	Gross Trading Profit .. £200
Transferred to Depreciation Fund £25	
£200	£200

B. Depreciation Fund

Added to Depreciation Fund £100	Transferred from Trading Profits £25
	Interest on Securities in the Fund £75
Total £100	Total £100

Method II
Combined Current Receipts and Outgoings

Available for Distribution to Shareholders £175	Gross Trading Profit .. £200
Depreciation Allowance .. £100	Interest from Securities .. £75
Total £275	Total £275

In what follows we shall use the term 'depreciation allowance' for the £100 in the above example which is taken from gross profits and interest on securities to add to the depreciation fund: we shall use the term 'transfer to depreciation fund' for the £25 which must be taken from profits and added to the £75 of interest from securities to make up the total addition to the depreciation fund of £100.

Now the essential thing is that over the ten years of our machine's life the sum of all the annual depreciation allowances should add up to the value of a new machine, namely to £1,000 in our example. There are, of course, an infinite number of ways in which this can be done. If a new machine costs £1,000 and lasts for ten years, a depreciation allowance of £100 in each year would add up to the necessary £1,000 at the end of the machine's life. This is often called the 'straight-line' method of depreciation.

Another method is to make a constant 'transfer to the depreciation fund' each year. If this method is adopted, the transfer to the depreciation fund need not be as much as £100 a year in order to accumulate £1,000 at the end of ten years because each sum transferred to the depreciation fund accumulates at compound interest; thus a constant 'transfer to the depreciation fund' involves a growing 'depreciation allowance' since the depreciation allowance is equal to the (constant) 'transfer to the depreciation fund' plus the interest on the (growing) depreciation fund accumulated up to date. We may call this the 'fixed-annuity' method of depreciation. The 'straight-line' depreciation involves a constant depreciation allowance throughout the life of the machine and the 'fixed-annuity' method involves a growing depreciation allowance throughout the life of the machine.

It is perfectly possible, of course, to have a system whereby the depreciation allowance falls as the machine becomes older. This could be exemplified by a system under which a depreciation allowance was made each year sufficient to write off a given percentage, say 20 per cent, of the book value of the machine each year. Thus suppose a machine cost £1,000. In the first year a depreciation allowance of £200 (or 20 per cent of £1,000) would be made and the book value of the machine would be written down to £800. In the second year a depreciation allowance of only £160 (or 20 per cent of £800) would be made and the book value of the machine would be written down by £160 from £800 to £640; and so on[1]. This may be called the 'diminishing-balance' method of depreciation. It is, of course, the method which would be fully appropriate if machinery depreciated by evaporation and not by sudden death.

Now in conditions of depreciation by sudden death the 'fixed-annuity' method of depreciation would appear to be the rational one. For this method is the one which will maintain the owner's net disposable income constant over the life of the machine. This is obvious. For if the machine will bring in a constant gross trading profit of £200 for each of its ten year's life, then the net profit enjoyed by the owner is kept constant over these years if the same constant sum is deducted from these trading profits for transfer to the depreciation fund[2]; and this is precisely the 'fixed-annuity' method of depreciation.

It can also be shown (see Appendix III, pages 174 and 175) that this 'fixed-annuity' method of depreciation is the one which, in conditions of depreciation by sudden death and of a constant rate of interest, will keep the owner's total capital at the same constant value over the length of life of the machine. With this method of depreciation, at every stage of the machine's life the loss of value in the machine itself due to its being nearer its death will just be offset by the growth of the depreciation fund. The value of the machine plus the value of the depreciation fund held against the machine will at every point in the machine's history be equal to the value of a new machine.

Thus the 'fixed-annuity' method for depreciation in the conditions which we are examining means that the value of the owner's total capital and the level of his net disposable income are

---

[1] With this system, however long one continues, there is, of course, always some remaining balance. Thus, if £1,000 is written down by 20 per cent each year in the way explained in the text, there would be a balance of £108 still at the end of 10 years, and if that marked the end of the machine's life, there would have to be a special once-for-all writing off of this amount in the tenth year. But if the percentage chosen for writing down the value of the machine each year is high and if the length of the machine's life is long, this becomes a negligible irregularity.

[2] In our numerical example a constant amount of £50 must be deducted from the constant gross profits of £200 each year, leaving a constant net disposable income for the owner of £150 each year. For a series of transfers of £50 each year for 10 years, each accumulated at compound interest of 15 per cent per annum, will together amount to £1,000 by the tenth year.

both maintained at a constant figure throughout the machine's life. This is not so with the other methods of depreciation. The 'straight-line' depreciation method means a larger depreciation allowance in the early years and a smaller depreciation allowance in the later years than does the 'fixed-annuity' depreciation method because the latter method means a rising depreciation allowance (equal to the fixed transfer to the depreciation fund plus the growing interest on securities held in the depreciation fund). It follows therefore, that with the 'straight-line' depreciation method, the net disposable income of the owner will rise over the life of the machine, and that the value of the owner's total capital will at first rise above the initial value of the machine and then in the later years of the machine's life fall back to this initial value. This rising trend of net disposable income over the life of the machine and this rise and subsequent fall in the total capital value of the owner will be even more marked with the 'diminishing-balance' method of depreciation, since the depreciation allowances in this case will actually fall over the life of the machine.

We have seen that a firm which owns the ageing machine should accumulate a depreciation fund against this machine to be able to replace this machine at the end of its ten-year life. In our particular numerical example, in the fifth year of the machine's life the machine, which was worth £1,000 when it was installed, will be worth only £666⅔ but the firm (on the 'fixed-annuity' method of depreciation) will have accumulated a depreciation fund of £333⅓. If the firm has invested this sum in securities it will have total assets of £1,000 (£666⅔ worth of machinery and £333⅓ worth of securities). Let us suppose that this firm financed itself in the first place by selling £1,000 of its own securities to the public and using this £1,000 to purchase its machine. In the fifth year of the life of the machine, then, the public still holds £1,000 of this firm's securities against which the firm holds £666⅔ worth of machinery plus £333⅓ *invested in some other firm's securities*[1]. This last item introduces an element of duplication for the economy as a whole which it is important not to disregard.

The net worth of all the securities held, not by firms, but by outside individual shareholders who are the ultimate owners of

---

[1] Since we are assuming no governmental finance, the only securities available on the market are those issued by other firms.

capital and recipients of income is not the value of the total assets held by all firms (i.e. the value of their machinery plus the value of their accumulated depreciation funds) but simply the value of the machinery owned by all firms. For in so far as a firm holds securities it must have bought up some shares issued by some other firms. The total of all shares issued by all firms will be equal to the total of all assets of all firms (machinery plus depreciation funds); but, of this total of all shares issued by all firms, an amount equal to the total of all firm's depreciation funds will be held by firms and not by individuals; the total of shares held by individuals will, therefore, equal the total of the value of all machinery held by firms.

The point becomes obvious if for the moment we make the assumption that all firms build up their depreciation funds by investing in their own securities. Then our single-machine firm in its initial year would have issued £1,000 securities to the public and have bought £1,000 worth of machinery. By the fifth year of the machine's life the firm would have re-bought and cancelled £333⅓ of its own securities (corresponding to its depreciation fund) leaving only £666⅔ of its securities held by the public against the £666⅔ worth of machinery which the firm now held. If all firms operated like this, no firm would ever hold any securities in a depreciation fund; the amount of securities issued by all firms together at any one time would always be equal to the value of all machinery at that time and these shares would all be held by individual shareholders.

In all essential respects for our purposes in this book this method of financing (using depreciation allowances to cancel one's own securities) and the other method (using depreciation allowances to invest in other firm's securities) come to exactly the same thing. In the fifth year of its life, with the former method the initial shareholders in our firm have £666⅔ of this firm's securities but have £333⅓ repaid to them which they will presumably have invested in the securities of other firms; with the latter method the initial shareholders will still have £1,000 of the firm's securities but this firm will now hold the £333⅓ of securities of other firms. With the former method of finance, the depreciation allowance (i.e. the amount of its own securities which are bought up and cancelled each year) grows each year under the 'fixed-annuity' principle because each year the firm uses to redeem its own shares a (fixed) sum of £50 plus the (growing) amount which it saves on interest payments to its ever diminishing shareholders; and with the latter method, the depreciation allowance (i.e. the amount it invests in the securities of other firms) grows each year because the firm adds to its depreciation fund the (fixed) 'transfer to the depreciation fund' of £50 plus the (growing) interest which it receives on the securities of other firms which it holds in its depreciation fund.

We have so far been considering the position of a firm which possesses a single machine. We will turn now to a firm possessing a set of machines. Such a firm can be regarded as the merger of a number of single-machine firms.

Let us turn to the consideration of a firm which possesses what we will call a 'balanced' set of machines[1]. In the case of our numerical example this means a firm possessing ten machines, of which one is new and has ten years to run, one is one year old and has nine years to run, one is two years old and has eight years to run, and so on. Now the value of a 'balanced' set of ten machines some old and some new, will clearly be less than the value of a set of machines all of which are new. Let us call a set of ten new machines a 'new set' and a 'balanced' set of ten machines of all ages a 'balanced set'.

If the rate of interest were zero, the value of a balanced set would be one half the value of a new set. Consider the array of machines in order of their age in a balanced set as shown in Diagram VI. Suppose first that the rate of interest were zero. This would mean that, since funds could be borrowed at a zero rate of interest, an owner of a machine would not mind whether his machine was going to produce its profit this year, next year, or the year after. He would be concerned with the size and value of its ultimate profit; he would prefer a profit of £200 to a profit of £100; but he would not mind if he got that profit this year or next year, since if he wanted to spend next year's profit this year he could borrow the necessary sum this year and repay it next year without interest out of next year's profit. In such circumstances the value of a machine would be strictly proportional to the number of years' life it had to run; a new machine with ten years to run would be capable of a future output five times as

---

[1] Following Champernowne and Kahn. *Loc. cit.*

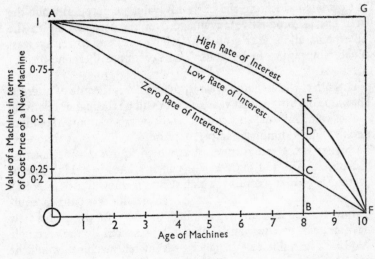

Diagram VI

great as that of an eight-year old machine with only two year's production left in it and would therefore be worth five times as much as an eight-year old machine, and so on. This proportional relationship between age and value is shown by the straight line in Diagram VI where BC = ⅕ × OA.

But suppose now that the rate of interest is positive. A profit of £200 this year is now worth more than a profit of £200 next year and still more than a profit of £200 the following year. An eight-year old machine will now be worth more than ⅕ of a new machine: next year's output will be the same for both machines and next year's output being only one year distant is the most valuable future output; the following year's output will also be the same for both machines and that year's output being only two years distant is the next most valuable output; it is true that in the following eight years the now new machine will produce an annual output while the now eight-year old machine will produce nothing, but these are the outputs of more distant future dates and their present value is less than that of the current outputs because of the rate of interest at which future values must be discounted. Thus the value of a machine with two more years to run is more than one fifth of that of a machine with ten more years to run; for the former shares with the latter the outputs of the two immediate future years (which are the currently valuable outputs) while the latter has its productive advantage over the former only in the subsequent eight year's output (which are the currently least valuable outputs). In Diagram VI BD is more than one-fifth of OA.

This effect is clearly the greater, the higher is the rate of interest. The value of the two next year's output will be the higher relatively to the value of the subsequent eight year's output, the more quickly values diminish simply because of distance in time—i.e. the higher is the rate of interest at which future income must be discounted. BE in Diagram VI (which relates to a high rate of interest) is greater than BD (which relates to a low rate of interest).

Now the value of a 'new set' of ten machines would in equilibrium be ten machines multiplied by the cost price of a new machine; and in Diagram VI this is represented by the rectangle OAGF. The value of a 'balanced set' of ten machines would be equal to the triangle OAF, if the rate of interest were zero; for, as we have seen, the value of each machine would fall off in exact proportion to its age. Now OAF is one-half OAGF. In other words, the value of a new set would be twice the value of a balanced set if the rate of interest were zero. At a low rate of interest the value of a balanced set would be equal to the area OADF and at a high rate of interest it would be equal to OAEF. In other words, the value of a balanced set would be less than that of a new set but greater than half that of a new set, the value of a balanced set being nearer the value of a new set the higher the rate of interest.

The relationship between the value of a balanced set and of a new set of machinery also depends upon the length of life of machines. Compound interest works in such a way that the present value of a future income falls off with increasing rapidity as the length of time which must elapse before it can be enjoyed increases. After a certain time the present value of a future income becomes more or less negligible. Now if machines last a very long time a balanced set of machines will consist, for the vast majority, of machines *all* of which are going to produce income for all the future years in which current income recipients are really at all interested. The present value of a balanced set will be almost equal to the present value of a new set. In the extreme limit, of course, in which machines last for ever there is literally no difference between the value of a balanced set and that of a new set of machines.

We can conclude this part of our discussion, therefore, by saying that with depreciation by sudden death a 'balanced set' of machines will be worth something between one-half and one times the value of a set of the same number of new machines, the balanced set approaching more closely in value the new set,

(i) the higher is the rate of interest and

(ii) the longer is the life of a machine[1].

In our numerical example in which the initial value of a machine is £1,000, the constant gross annual profit on it £200, its length of life 10 years, and the rate of interest 15 per cent per annum, a set of ten new machines would be worth £10,000 but a balanced set of ten machines of all ages would be worth only two-thirds of this or £6,666⅔.

Now a firm with such a balanced set of machines might have been built up by two different methods of finance. In both cases in the initial year the firm would have issued £1,000 of its own securities to purchase its first machine; and in the next year it would have earned £200 on this machine, would have made a depreciation allowance on the first machine of £50, would have distributed £150 in net profits, and would have spent £1,000 in buying another machine. But there are two ways in which it might have dealt with its depreciation fund and with the finance of the second machine.

(i) In the first case, it would issue in the second year only £950 of new securities and would have added the £50 depreciation allowance on the first machine to this sum to make up the £1,000 needed for the purchase of a machine in the second year. If it went on in this way building up a balanced set of machines over the first ten years of its life by investing its depreciation allowances in its own additional machinery, it would end up by having issued £6,666⅔ of securities and owning £6,666⅔ worth of machinery.

---

[1] From the formula reached by Champernowne and Kahn and reproduced in Appendix III of this book (see page 176 below) it can be seen that the value of a new set relatively to the value of a balanced set depends upon the product (IT) of the rate of interest (I) and the length of life of the machine (T), the value of a balanced set approaching one-half of the value of a new set as IT approaches zero and the value of a balanced set approaching the value of a new set as IT approaches infinity.

It would be making a gross profit of £2,000 a year (i.e. a gross profit of £200 on each of 10 machines) and making a depreciation allowance each year of £1,000 (reckoned on the 'fixed-annuity' principle for each machine separately); this depreciation allowance would be just sufficient to purchase one new machine each year to replace the ten-year old machine in its stock, and its net profit distributed to shareholders would be £2,000 *minus* the depreciation allowance of £1,000; and this net profit of £1,000 would represent 15 per cent on the total outstanding securities of £6,666⅔.

(ii) In the second case, in each of the first ten years of its life the firm would have issued £1,000 of its own securities to purchase an additional machine. In this case it would have accumulated a depreciation fund on its existing machines by investing the depreciation allowances each year in the securities of other firms. In this case after the tenth year of its build-up the firm would have issued £10,000 of its own securities; it would own machinery worth £6,666⅔ but, in addition, it would also own securities of other firms worth £3,333⅓. It would as before have £2,000 in income from gross profits, but it would now also have an income of £500 (15 per cent on £3,333⅓) from interest on other firms' securities. From this gross income of £2,500 it would, as before, deduct £1,000 a year in depreciation allowance (which, as before, would just meet the annual cost of replacing one machine); and the £1,500 which it would be able to distribute to its own shareholders would represent 15 per cent on their shareholding of £10,000.

But, as we have already seen, there is no essential difference between these situations except that in situation (i) the shareholders of the firm will hold £6,666⅔ of this firm's and £3,333⅓ of other firms' securities whereas in situation (ii) they will hold £10,000 of this firm's securities and this firm in turn will hold the £3,333⅓ of other firms' securities.

Let us next consider a firm which is growing in the sense that the amount it spends on gross investment (i.e. on machinery for replacement of old machinery and for addition to its stock of machinery) grows and has been growing for some time at a constant proportionate rate. If, for example, the rate of growth of gross investment were 5 per cent per annum, and in year 1 it spent £1,000 on machinery, then in year 2 it would spend £1,050 (or

£1,000 × 1·05) on machinery, in year 3 it would spend £1,102½ (or £1,050 × 1·05) on machinery, and so on. Suppose that it has been growing like this for at least ten years, the length of life of a machine. It will now have an 'unbalanced' set of machines in the sense that the number purchased nine years ago will be 5 per cent less than the number purchased eight years ago, which will be 5 per cent less than the number purchased seven years ago, and so on. The age-distribution of its stock of machines will be abnormal and will be weighted in favour of the younger machines. Such a firm would be representative of a whole economy which had reached a state of steady economic growth.

The amount which such a steadily growing firm will need to spend on replacement in any one year will be less than the total depreciation allowances which it will make that year. This can readily be seen. The replacement expenditure this year is only the relative small sum needed to replace the relatively small number of machines installed ten years ago. But the depreciation allowances are made in respect of all machines including the relatively large number of new machines which will not need replacement for many years. We know that, with any depreciation method, if the age-distribution of the stock of machines were normal, the total depreciation allowance made in respect of all machines would be just sufficient to replace the machine which collapsed each year, because every depreciation method must be such as to make the sum of the depreciation allowances made in each year of a machine's life equal to the cost of that machine. It follows that with an abnormally small number of old machines (which need replacement) and an abnormally large number of new machines (which contribute to the depreciation allowance but do not need replacement), depreciation allowances will exceed replacement expenditures. The accumulating depreciation funds of businesses may thus in a growing economy in which machines depreciate by sudden death rather than by evaporation in fact contribute quite a substantial amount to the 'savings' required to finance additions to the community's stock of machinery.

In a steadily growing economy with depreciation by sudden death, depreciation allowances will thus exceed replacement allowances, whatever method of depreciation is adopted. But if the 'straight-line' method rather than the 'fixed-annuity' method of depreciation is adopted, the excess of depreciation allowances over replacement will be even more marked; for with the former method the depreciation allowance in respect of any one machine remains constant throughout that machine's life, whereas with the latter method the depreciation allowance grows as the depreciation fund accumulates. With the former method, therefore, a greater depreciation allowance is made in respect of young machines, and a smaller depreciation allowance is made in respect of old machines, than with the latter. The former method will, therefore, accentuate the divergence between depreciation and replacement since with the former method not only are there an abnormally large number of young machines not needing replacement but the depreciation allowance made in respect of each young machine is abnormally high. *A fortiori*, this divergence would be still more marked in the case of the 'diminishing-balance' method of depreciation; for in this case the depreciation allowance actually falls as the machine grows older so that the young machines make a still higher contribution to the total depreciation allowance.

In Appendix III formulae are given whereby this divergence can be calculated in the case of the 'fixed-annuity' and the 'straight-line' methods of depreciation. If we suppose that machines last ten years, that the rate of interest is 15 per cent per annum, and that the amount of gross investment in machinery grows at 5 per cent per annum, then in the case of the 'fixed-annuity' method of depreciation depreciation allowances will be practically 20 per cent, and with the 'straight-line' method they will be more than 25 per cent, greater than is necessary to meet replacement each year[1].

---

[1] Throughout this book we are reckoning in terms of a money which maintains a constant purchasing power in terms of consumption goods. If, however, depreciation allowances are fixed in money terms according to the initial money cost of the machinery concerned and if there is a continuous inflation of prices, depreciation allowances will *pro tanto* be reduced in terms of current purchasing power over new machines. This inflationary effect could, of course, easily swamp the real effect examined in the text (see E. D. Domar *loc. cit.*).

APPENDIX I

One Product and Three Factors

(I) CHANGES IN THE DISTRIBUTION OF INCOME

Consider the proportion of income going to wages, $Q = \dfrac{WL.}{Y}$

If we differentiate this expression, we have

$$q = w + l + y \qquad \ldots (1)$$

We can substitute into (1) the value of y from our basic relationship as given on page 12, namely

$$y = Uk + Ql + r \qquad \ldots (2)$$

In order to see from (1) what is happening to the proportion of income going to wages in terms of changes in the factor supplies (k and l) and in technical knowledge (r, r_l, etc.), it remains to see what is happening to the wage rate (w).

Consider a constant-returns production function

$$Y = F(K, L, N, t) \qquad \ldots (3)$$

We will write the marginal products of the factors K, L, and N $\left(\dfrac{\partial Y}{\partial K}\right)$ etc. as F_k etc., and the partial derivatives of the marginal products $\dfrac{\partial^2 Y}{\partial K^2}$, $\dfrac{\partial^2 Y}{\partial K \partial L}$ etc.) as F_{kk}, F_{kl} etc. It is to be remembered that $F_{kl} = F_{lk}$ etc.

Since the wage rate (W) is equal to the marginal product of labour (l) we have

$$w = \frac{1}{W}\frac{dW}{dt} = \frac{1}{W}\{LF_{ll} + KF_{lk}k\} + r \qquad \ldots (4)$$

where $r_l = \dfrac{1}{F}\dfrac{\partial F_l}{\partial t}$ or the proportionate rate of rise in the marginal product of labour due solely to the passage of time and technical progress.

93

We must next consider the terms F_{ll} and F_{lk} in equation (4). Consider a state of affairs in which t is constant so that technical knowledge is unchanged, but in which there are small changes in all three factors of production K, L, and N. By differentiation of the production function in equation (3) we have

$$dY = F_k \, dK + F_l \, dL + F_n \, dN \qquad \ldots (5)$$

and this relationship is true for all values of dK, dL, and dN.

Moreover since the production function is homogeneous of the first degree we have

$$Y = F_k K + F_l L + F_n N \qquad \ldots (6)$$

and by differentiation of (6) we have

$$\left. \begin{aligned}
dY = \ &K(F_{kk} \, dK + F_{kl} \, dL + F_{kn} \, dN) \\
&+ L(F_{lk} \, dK + F_{ll} \, dL + F_{ln} \, dN) \\
&+ N(F_{nk} \, dK + F_{nl} \, dL + F_{nn} \, dN) \\
&+ F_k \, dK + F_l \, dL + F_n \, dN
\end{aligned} \right\} \qquad \ldots (7)$$

which is also true for all values of dK, dL, and dN.

If one subtracts (5) and (7) one has

$$o = dK(KF_{kk} + LF_{lk} + NF_{nk}) + dL(KF_{kl} + LF_{ll} + NF_{nl}) + \\ + dN(KF_{kn} + LF_{ln} + NF_{nn}).$$

Since this relationship must be true for all values of dK, dL, and dN, we can conclude that

$$\left. \begin{aligned}
KF_{kk} &= -LF_{kl} - NF_{kn} \\
LF_{ll} &= -KF_{kl} - NF_{ln} \\
NF_{nn} &= -KF_{kn} - LF_{ln}
\end{aligned} \right\} \qquad \ldots (8)$$

and

If now we substitute the value of F_{ll} from the second equation in (8) into equation (4) and then substitute the value of w from (4) and of y from (2) into equation (1) we obtain

$$q = -(k-l)\left(U - \frac{K}{W}F_{kl} \right) + l\left(Z - \frac{N}{W}F_{ln} \right) + \beta_l \qquad \ldots (9)$$

where $\beta_l = r_l - r$.

By symmetry we have

$$u = -(l-k)\left(Q - \frac{L}{V}F_{kl} \right) + k\left(Z - \frac{N}{V}F_{kn} \right) + \beta_k$$

which can be rearranged as

$$u = (k-l)\left(Z - \frac{N}{V}F_{kn} + Q - \frac{L}{V}F_{kl}\right) + l\left(Z - \frac{N}{V}F_{kn}\right) + \beta_k \ldots (10)$$

Let us consider the significance of the terms on the right-hand side of the expression for q in equation (9). β_l is a straightforward term expressing the extent to which a labour-using bias in technical progress will tend to raise the proportion of the national income going to wages.

The other terms express the effect of changes in factor proportions upon the distribution of income between the factors. With constant returns to scale it is only the proportions between the factors, and not the absolute amount of the factors, which will affect the distribution of income If then there is a proportionate increase in the supply of labour of l and of machinery of k with no change in the supply of land, the effect of this upon marginal products and so upon the distribution of income is exactly the same as the effect of a proportionate reduction in the supply of land of l and a proportionate increase in the supply of machinery of $(k-l)$ with no change in the supply of labour. The term $-(k-l)\left(U - \frac{K}{W}F_{kl}\right)$ thus marks the effect of an increase in the supply of machinery in lowering or raising the proportion of the national income going to wages. Whether an increase in machinery will raise or lower Q depends upon the substitutability between the factors of production. If machinery is a very good substitute for the other factors, an increase in the supply of machinery will have very little effect in lowering profits per machine or in raising the wage per worker; and it will, therefore, cause a rise in the share of income going to profits and a fall in the share going to wages. And conversely, if the elasticity of substitution between machinery and labour is very low, this in itself will tend to make an increase in the supply of machinery cause a very large fall in profits per machine and a very large rise in the wage per worker; and in this case the share of profits will fall and of wages will rise. $\frac{K}{W}F_{kl}$ which equals $\frac{K}{W}\frac{\partial W}{\partial K}$ measures this substitution factor. If substitutability is small, then this term will be large because a small proportionate increase in K will cause a large proportionate rise in W.

Similarly, the term $l\left(Z - \dfrac{N}{W}F_{ln}\right)$ on the right-hand side of equation (9) measures the effect of a fall in the amount of land per worker in raising the share of income going to wages. $\dfrac{N}{W}F_{ln} = \dfrac{N}{W}\dfrac{\partial W}{\partial N}$; and if this is greater than Z, then a fall in the amount of land per head will lower the share of income going to wages. $\dfrac{N}{W}\dfrac{\partial W}{\partial N}$ will tend to be large if the elasticity of substitution between land and labour is small, so that a small reduction in the supply of land causes a large fall in the demand for labour and so in the wage rate.

The terms like $\dfrac{K}{W}F_{kl}\left(= \dfrac{W}{K}\dfrac{\partial K}{\partial W}\right)$ and $\dfrac{N}{W}F_{ln}\left(= \dfrac{N}{W}\dfrac{\partial W}{\partial N}\right)$ thus depend upon the elasticities of substitution between the factors of production, but unfortunately the dependence is a little more complicated than might at first sight appear. The term $\dfrac{W}{K}\dfrac{\partial W}{\partial K}$, for example, measures the percentage increase in the marginal product of labour which would be caused by a one per cent increase in the amount of machinery available to be employed in a given state of technical knowledge with a given amount of land and labour. The fundamental consideration in determining the value of $\dfrac{K}{W}\dfrac{\partial W}{\partial K}$ is, therefore, the elasticity of substitution between labour and machinery, σ_{kl}. If these two factors are very good substitutes, it will be easy to employ more machinery without demanding much more labour and driving the wage rate up; $\dfrac{K}{W}\dfrac{\partial W}{\partial K}$ will tend to be low if σ_{kl} is high and *vice versa*. But this is not the end of the matter. Suppose that labour and machinery are good substitutes. Then an increase in the amount of machinery will not raise the marginal product of labour much; but there will now be an increase in the amount of labour-plus-machinery to be employed with a given amount of land. If labour and machinery are bad substitutes for land, then the wage per worker and the profit per machine will have to be lowered and the rent per acre raised in order to get the increased amount of labour-plus-machinery employed with the given amount of land. Indeed, if labour and machinery were very good substitutes for each other but both were very bad substitutes for land, the net effect of the increased supply of machinery might be a fall in the marginal product of labour as well as that of machinery. $\dfrac{K}{W}\dfrac{\partial W}{\partial K}$ will therefore be high in so far as σ_{kl} is low and will be low (and even negative) in so far as the elasticities of substitution between machinery and land and between labour and land (σ_{kn} and σ_{ln}) are low.

Our next task is to express the terms F_{lk} etc. in terms of the three elasticities of substitution, σ_{nl}, σ_{nk}, and σ_{lk}. The best method of defining and measuring these elasticities of substitution has been discussed above (page 32). Here it is sufficient to remind the reader that the elasticity of substitution between men and machinery, for example, is defined as the percentage increase in the ratio of machinery to men which would be necessary to cause a 1 per cent decline in the ratio of profits per machine to wages per worker, when (i) the amount of the third factor, land, is kept constant, (ii) the increase in the amount of machinery is just sufficient to offset the reduction in the amount of labour in its effect on production, and (iii) the factors are paid rewards equal to their marginal products.

We can write then

$$\sigma_{kl} = -\frac{(\mathrm{d}K/K)-(\mathrm{d}L/L)}{(\mathrm{d}F_k/F_k)-(\mathrm{d}F_l/F_l)} \qquad \ldots (11)$$

when $\mathrm{d}K$, $\mathrm{d}L$, $\mathrm{d}F_k$ and $\mathrm{d}F_l$ have the values which they would have when $\mathrm{d}Y = \mathrm{d}N = 0$. From equation (5) we know that when output and the amount of land are constant ($\mathrm{d}Y = \mathrm{d}N = 0$), then

$$\mathrm{d}L = -\frac{F_k}{F_l}\,\mathrm{d}K. \qquad \ldots (12)$$

By differentiation of F_l we have, when $\mathrm{d}N = 0$,

$$\mathrm{d}F_l = F_{kl}\,\mathrm{d}K + F_{ll}\,\mathrm{d}L$$

or from the second equation in (8) and from (12)

$$\mathrm{d}F_l = \mathrm{d}K\left\{F_{lk}\left(1+\frac{F_kK}{F_lL}\right)+F_{ln}\frac{F_kN}{F_lL}\right\}$$

and similarly

$$\mathrm{d}F_k = -\mathrm{d}K\left\{F_{lk}\left(\frac{L}{K}+\frac{F_k}{F_l}\right)+F_{nk}\frac{N}{K}\right\} \qquad \left.\right\} \ldots (13)$$

If now we substitute the value of dL from (12) and of dF_l and dF_k from (13) into (11), re-arrange terms, and write $F_k K = UY$ etc., we get:

$$\frac{1}{\sigma_{kl}} = \frac{KL}{(U+Q)Y}\left\{ F_{kl}\left(2+\frac{U}{Q}+\frac{Q}{U}\right) + F_{ln}\frac{N}{K}\frac{U}{Q} + F_{nk}\frac{N}{L}\frac{Q}{U}\right\}$$

By symmetry we can also deduce that:

$$\frac{1}{\sigma_{kn}} = \frac{KN}{(U+Z)Y}\left\{ F_{kn}\left(2+\frac{U}{Z}+\frac{Z}{U}\right) + F_{nl}\frac{L}{K}\frac{U}{Z} + F_{kl}\frac{L}{N}\frac{Z}{U}\right\}$$

and

$$\frac{1}{\sigma_{ln}} = \frac{LN}{(Q+Z)Y}\left\{ F_{ln}\left(2+\frac{Q}{Z}+\frac{Z}{Q}\right) + F_{lk}\frac{K}{N}\frac{Z}{Q} + F_{nk}\frac{K}{L}\frac{Q}{Z}\right\}$$

$$\cdots (14)$$

The three equations in (14) give us three relationships for the three terms F_{kl}, F_{nl}, and F_{kn}. If we solve equations (14) for these three terms we get:

$$F_{kl}\left(\equiv \frac{\partial W}{\partial K} \equiv \frac{\partial V}{\partial L}\right) = \frac{Y}{2KL}\left\{\frac{(U+Q)[(1-Q)(1-U)+UQ]}{\sigma_{kl}} - \frac{Q(1-Q)(1-2U)}{\sigma_{nk}} - \frac{U(1-U)(1-2Q)}{\sigma_{nl}}\right\}$$

$$F_{kn}\left(\equiv \frac{\partial V}{\partial N} \equiv \frac{\partial G}{\partial K}\right) = \frac{Y}{2KN}\left\{\frac{(U+Z)[(1-Z)(1-U)+UZ]}{\sigma_{kn}} - \frac{Z(1-Z)(1-2U)}{\sigma_{lk}} - \frac{U(1-U)(1-2Z)}{\sigma_{nl}}\right\}$$

$$F_{nl}\left(\equiv \frac{\partial W}{\partial N} \equiv \frac{\partial G}{\partial L}\right) = \frac{Y}{2NL}\left\{\frac{(Z+Q)[(1-Q)(1-Z)+QZ]}{\sigma_n} - \frac{Q(1-Q)(1-2Z)}{\sigma_{nk}} - \frac{Z(1-Z)(1-2Q)}{\sigma_{kl}}\right\}$$

$$\cdots (15)$$

It would be possible to substitute the values of F_{kl}, F_{kn}, and F_{nl} from (15) into equations (9) and (10) and thus obtain the values of q and u in terms of σ_{nk}, σ_{nl}, and σ_{kl}. But the formulae are much too clumsy to handle. It may, however, be useful to consider some special cases.

Case i. Suppose that all three factors receive the same proportion of the national income, i.e. that their proportional marginal products are equal so that $U = Q = Z = \frac{1}{3}$. Then by simplification of (15) and substitution for F_{kl}, F_{kn}, and F_{nl} into (9) and (10) we get

$$
\left.
\begin{aligned}
q = & -(k-l)\frac{1}{3}\left\{1 - \frac{1}{3}\left[\frac{5}{\sigma_{kl}} - \frac{1}{\sigma_{nk}} - \frac{1}{\sigma_{nl}}\right]\right\} + \\
& + l\frac{1}{3}\left\{1 - \frac{1}{3}\left[\frac{5}{\sigma_{nl}} - \frac{1}{\sigma_{nk}} - \frac{1}{\sigma_{kl}}\right]\right\} + \beta_l \\[6pt]
u = & (k-l)\frac{2}{3}\left\{1 - \frac{1}{3}\left[\frac{2}{\sigma_{kn}} + \frac{2}{\sigma_{kl}} - \frac{1}{\sigma_{ln}}\right]\right\} + \\
& + l\frac{1}{3}\left\{1 - \frac{1}{3}\left[\frac{5}{\sigma_{kn}} - \frac{1}{\sigma_{kl}} - \frac{1}{\sigma_{nl}}\right]\right\} + \beta_k
\end{aligned}
\right\} \quad \dots (16)
$$

Case ii. Suppose that all the elasticities of substitution are equal, i.e. that $\sigma_{nk} = \sigma_{nl} = \sigma_{kl} = \sigma$. Then by simplification of (15) and substitution for F_{kl}, F_{kn}, and F_{nl} into (9) and (10) we get

$$
\left.
\begin{aligned}
q = & -(k-l)U\frac{\sigma-1}{\sigma} + lZ\frac{\sigma-1}{\sigma} + \beta_l \\
u = & (k-l)(Q+Z)\frac{\sigma-1}{\sigma} + lZ\frac{\sigma-1}{\sigma} + \beta_k
\end{aligned}
\right\} \quad \dots (17)
$$

Case iii. If we write $\sigma = 1$ in equations (17) we obtain

$$
\left.
\begin{aligned}
q = \beta_l \\
u = \beta_k
\end{aligned}
\right\} \quad \dots (18)
$$

which shows that if all elasticities of substitution were equal to unity, then changes in the supplies of the factors will have no effect upon the proportion of the national income which is paid in wages. Only a bias in the nature of inventions could change the distribution of income.

Case iv. If we allow all the σ's to approach infinity in equations (17) we obtain

$$
\left.
\begin{aligned}
q = & -(k-l)U + lZ + \beta_l \\
u = & (k-l)(Q+Z) + lZ + \beta_k
\end{aligned}
\right\} \quad \dots (19)
$$

Case v. Finally if we allowed all the σ's to approach zero, we would either reach a position in which the distribution of income was indeterminate (i.e. the factors happened to be supplied in exactly the proportions in which they were needed in production) or else a position in which one or two of the factors were paid nothing (if either one or two factors were in greater supply relatively to the third factor than the proportions in which they were needed for production).

(2) CHANGES IN THE RATE OF ECONOMIC GROWTH

Our basic expression for the growth rate of the national product can be expressed as $y = Uk + Ql + r$ (see equation (2)). It is the purpose of this section to investigate the sign of $\dfrac{dy}{dt}$, i.e. to ask whether the growth rate y will be rising or falling as time passes. Let us assume that l and r are constant. If we then differentiate equation (2) we obtain:

$$\frac{dy}{dt} = Uk\frac{1}{k}\frac{dk}{dt} + Uku + Qlq \qquad \ldots (20)$$

where $u = \dfrac{1}{U}\dfrac{dU}{dt}$ and similarly for q.

Now we know that $k = \dfrac{SY}{K}$ since the rate of capital accumulation k is equal to the ratio of new savings to the capital stock. If we differentiate this expression for k we have $\dfrac{1}{k}\dfrac{dk}{dt} = s + y - k$ and if we substitute in this for y from (2) we have

$$\frac{1}{k}\frac{dk}{dt} = s - (1 - U)k + Ql + r \qquad \ldots (21)$$

Let us write $S = S_v U + S_w Q + S_g Z$ (see page 33) and assume that S_v, S_w, and S_g are all constant. Let us assume further that $S_v = S_g$ and write $\gamma = S_v - S_w$. Then, since $U + Q + Z = 1$, we have $S = S_v - \gamma Q$ so that by differentiation

$$s = -\frac{\gamma Q}{S}q. \qquad \ldots (22)$$

By elimination of the four terms q, u, s, and $\dfrac{1}{k}\dfrac{dk}{dt}$ between the five equations (9), (10), (20), (21), and (22) we obtain

$$\frac{dy}{dt} = VS(Uk+Ql+r-k) \tag{a}$$

$$+\gamma QV\left\{\left(U-\frac{K}{W}F_{lk}\right)(k-l)-\left(Z-\frac{N}{W}F_{ln}\right)l-\beta_l\right\} \tag{b}$$

$$+Q\left(U-\frac{K}{W}F_{lk}\right)(k-l)^2+U\left(Z-\frac{N}{V}F_{nk}\right)k^2+$$

$$+Q\left(Z-\frac{N}{W}F_{ln}\right)l^2 \tag{c}$$

$$+U\beta_k k+Q\beta_l l. \tag{d}$$

$$\dots (23)$$

Let us, by way of example, consider this in the case shown in equations (17), when $\sigma_{nk} = \sigma_{nl} = \sigma_{kl} = \sigma$. We have then

$$\frac{dy}{dt} = VS(Uk+Ql+r-k) \tag{a}$$

$$+\gamma VQ\left\{\frac{\sigma-1}{\sigma}(U[k-l]-Zl)-\beta_l\right\} \tag{b}$$

$$+\frac{\sigma-1}{\sigma}\{UQ(k-l)^2+Z(Uk^2+Ql^2)\} \tag{c}$$

$$+U\beta_k k+Q\beta_l l. \tag{d}$$

$$\dots (24)$$

The four lines (a), (b), (c), and (d) of equations (23) or (24) express the four main sets of influences which will together decide whether the growth rate of the national product is rising or falling. Let us consider these four influences in turn in terms of the special case expressed in equation (24) when all the elasticities of substitution are the same.

(a) Since $Uk+Ql+r = y$, the first element in $\dfrac{dy}{dt}$ is $VS(y-k)$. This is >0, if $y > k$. If $y > k$, then the ratio $\dfrac{Y}{K}$ is rising. Since

$k = \dfrac{SY}{K}$, a rise in $\dfrac{Y}{K}$ (with any given level of S) tends to raise k.

But a rise in the rate of capital accumulation k will tend to raise y, since $y = Uk + Ql + r$. In other words if Ql and r are large (so that the national product will be growing rapidly in any case) and if the proportion of income saved is small so that k is low, then the ratio of income to capital will be rising, hence the ratio of total savings to capital stock will tend to be rising, hence the rate of capital accumulation will tend to be rising, and hence the growth rate in the national product will tend to be rising. This is the influence on changes in y which is discussed at length in pages 25 and 26 in the main text.

(b) The rate of capital accumulation may be growing not only because the ratio of income to capital is growing but because the proportion of income saved is rising. The element (b) is equation (24) expresses this possibility. In our present model the proportion of income saved can increase only if there is a shift in the division of the national income away from wages (of which a relatively small proportion is assumed to be saved) on to profits and rents (of which a larger proportion is supposed to be saved). γ, the difference between these savings proportions, measures the potential importance of this influence. Now there are two reasons why there may be a shift of income from wages to profits and rents. First, if the elasticities of substitution between the factors of production are great ($\sigma > 1$), an accumulation of capital more rapid than the growth of the working population ($k > l$) will cause a shift from wages to profits, provided that this is not offset by any shift of income from rents to wages as labour grows relatively to the available land (i.e. provided that $Zl < U[k-l]$). Second, if inventions are labour-saving (i.e. if $\beta_l < 0$) there will be a further force at work shifting income from wages to profits and rents and so raising the ratio of income saved.

(c) The influence in row (c) of equation (24) expresses the important fact that high elasticities of substitution ($\sigma > 1$) between the factors of production themselves exert an important influence in accelerating the growth rate of the national product. If $\sigma > 1$, then provided k and/or l are not zero, this element is bound to exert a positive influence on $\dfrac{dy}{dt}$. The reason for this important result is simple. Suppose that capital is being accumulated relatively to labour and land. Then if $\sigma > 1$, a larger and larger proportion of the national income will be going to profits. U will be rising. But U measures not only the proportion of the national income going to profits but also (see page 11 of the main text) the proportionate marginal product of capital. In other words, if capital is growing more rapidly than labour and land, capital will be becoming a more and more important factor in causing economic growth, i.e. a 1 per cent increase in the stock of capital will be leading to a larger and larger percentage increase in output. Now exactly the same argument could be applied to the growth of population. If labour were growing relatively to land and capital, and if labour were a very good substitute for capital and land in production, its relative importance as a factor of production would be growing and a given rate of growth of population would be causing an ever greater rate of rise in the total national product. High elasticities of substitution between the factors of production tend to cause the growth rate of the national product to increase if any changes in factor proportions are taking place in the process of growth.

(d) Row (d) in equation (24) expresses a similar sort of effect of a bias in the nature of technical progress. Thus suppose that capital accumulation is taking place ($k > 0$) without any increase in the supply of labour ($l = 0$); and suppose further that the nature of technical progress is capital-using ($\beta_k > 0$). Then element (d) will be positive and will be tending to raise the growth rate of the national income. For invention is making more and more productive at the margin that particular factor of production which, through its growth, is the cause of the growth of the national product. Suppose capital accumulation to be the only cause of growth. A given rate of capital accumulation (a given k) may be leading to an ever higher rate of growth of output *either* (row c) because capital is a very good substitute for land and labour so that capital as it accumulates is becoming relatively more and more important as a factor of production *or else* (row (d)) simply because the nature of technical progress is such as to make it relatively more and more important as a factor of production.

If in considering row (d) we allow for the fact that labour may be growing as well as capital accumulating, we must allow for the fact that β_k and β_l are not wholly independent of each other. It is only in so far as technical progress is very land-saving that it could be both capital-using and labour-using (i.e. both β_k and $\beta_l > 0$). Consider any production function $X = F(K, L, N)$. If there are constant returns to scale, we have by Euler's theorem

$X = X_k K + X_l L + X_n N$ where $X_k = \dfrac{\partial X}{\partial K}$ etc. Let us now keep

X, L, and N constant but allow technical progress to take place with the passage of time. Then by differentiating the above expression for X we have

$$\frac{1}{X}\frac{\partial X}{\partial t} = \frac{X_k K}{X}\frac{1}{X_k}\frac{\partial X_k}{\partial t} + \frac{X_l L}{X}\frac{1}{X_l}\frac{\partial X_l}{\partial t} + \frac{X_n N}{X}\frac{1}{X_n}\frac{\partial X_n}{\partial t}$$

or $\qquad r = \qquad Qr_l \qquad + \qquad Ur_k \qquad + \qquad Zr_n$

since $\dfrac{1}{X}\dfrac{\partial X}{\partial t}$ is the rate of technical progress r and $\dfrac{1}{X_l}\dfrac{\partial X_l}{\partial t}$ measures the proportionate rate of growth of the marginal product of labour resulting from technical progress, r_l, and so on.

By definition $\beta_l = r_l - r$, $\beta_k = r_k - r$, and $\beta_n = r_n - r$. Remembering that $Q + U + Z = 1$ we have

$$Q\beta_l + U\beta_k + Z\beta_n = 0.$$

We can now write row (d) of equation (26) as

$$-(k-l)\frac{QU}{U+Q}\beta - (Uk+Ql)\frac{Z}{U+Q}\beta_n \qquad \ldots (25)$$

where $\beta = \beta_l - \beta_k$ or the extent to which inventions are labour-using relatively to capital-using. If capital accumulation is more rapid than population growth $(k-l)$ and inventions are labour-using relatively to capital-using ($\beta > 0$), this will be a factor slowing down the rate of growth of income because inventions will be making the fast-growing factor less productive at the margin than the slow growing factor At the same time if both capital and population are growing, while land is constant, and if inventions are land-using ($\beta_n > 0$), there will be a further slowing down of the growth rate of national product because inventions are making the stationary factor land more and more important in production at the margin.

If $Z = 0$ so that $U + Q = 1$ and we are dealing with only the two factors, capital and labour, then we can rewrite the expression at (25) as

$$\left.\begin{array}{c} -(k-l)Q(1-Q)\beta \\ -(k-l)Q\beta_l \\ +(k-l)(1-Q)\beta_k \end{array}\right\} \qquad \ldots (26)$$

or

or

If an invention is labour-using it must now be capital saving and *vice versa*. We can use β_l or β_k or $\beta(=\beta_l-\beta_k)$ as the unique measure of the bias in inventions. For the reasons explained in the last paragraph the growth rate will be tending to fall if capital is accumulating more rapidly than population is growing and inventions are capital-saving or if population is growing more rapidly than capital is being accumulated and inventions are labour-saving.

We can now take certain special values of some of the parameters in equations (23) and (24) and derive two special cases which we discussed in Chapters 3 and 4 of the main text.

If first we assume that $\sigma = 1$ and $\beta_l = \beta_k = \beta_n = 0$, we have the case where the proportionate distribution of income between the factors of production is constant. Rows (b), (c), and (d) of equation (24) disappear and we are left only with row (a) of the equation. In Chapter 4 we show that in these conditions of constant proportions of income going to the three factors we shall always end up with the situation in which $y = k$ (i.e. the rate of growth of national income is equal to the rate of growth of the capital stock). But since $y = Uk+Ql+r$, the element in row (a) on the right-hand side of equation (24) also becomes zero when $y = k$. In other words $\dfrac{dy}{dt} = 0$ and we have the case of steady growth examined in Chapter 4.

Let us next consider the special case which is examined on pages 22 to 25 of Chapter 3 in the main text. We were assuming there that the population was constant and that the proportion of income saved was also constant. Let us, therefore, write $l = \gamma = 0$ in equation (24). Remembering that $k = \dfrac{SY}{K}$, that $VK = UY$, and that $\beta_k = r_k - r$ we then have

$$\frac{dy}{dt} = VS\left(r_k - \frac{SY}{K}\left[\frac{N}{V}F_{nk} + \frac{L}{V}F_{lk}\right]\right). \qquad \ldots (27)$$

From the first equation in (8) we see that equation (27) could be written

$$\frac{dy}{dt} = VS\left(r_k - \frac{SY}{K}\frac{1}{\epsilon_k}\right) \qquad \ldots (28)$$

where $\epsilon_k = -\dfrac{V}{KF_{kk}} = -\dfrac{V}{K}\dfrac{\partial K}{\partial V}$ and measures the numerical value of the elasticity of demand for machinery (i.e. in the sense of the percentage increase in the amount of machinery which would be employed with a given amount of land and labour if the charge for hiring a machine fell by 1 per cent).

An alternative expression for equation (27) can be obtained by substituting into (27) for F_{nk} and F_{lk} from equations (15). We then have

$$\frac{dy}{dt} = VS\left(r_k - \frac{SY}{K}[1-U]\left[\frac{1-Z}{\sigma_{kl}} + \frac{1-Q}{\sigma_{kn}} - \frac{U}{\sigma_{nl}}\right]\right) \quad \ldots (29)$$

Starting with any given position (i.e. with any given Y and K) this is more likely to be positive (i) the greater is r_k, i.e. the greater and more machine-using is technical progress, (ii) the greater are σ_{kl} and σ_{kn}, and (iii) the smaller is S[1].

This last condition does not imply that an increase in the proportion of income saved will always mean a decrease in the rate at which the growth rate of the national income is rising; it means only that (with S a positive figure) the growth rate of the national income will be increasing if S is below a certain figure and will be falling if S is above a certain figure. We can see the relationship between $\dfrac{dy}{dt}$ (the rate at which the growth rate of income is itself rising) and the level of S in the following way.

With our present assumption that population is constant we have $y = VS+r$. Since S and r are also both assumed to be constant, we have $\dfrac{dy}{dt} = S\dfrac{dV}{dt}$. Combining this with equation (28) we have

$$\frac{dy}{dt} = S\frac{dV}{dt} = S\left(Vr_k - \frac{V}{\epsilon_k}\frac{SY}{K}\right) \qquad \ldots (30)$$

---

[1] The reason for these conditions are discussed on page 24 of the main text.

In this equation Vr_k measures the amount by which the marginal product of machinery is being raised because of technical progress and $\dfrac{V}{\epsilon_k}\dfrac{SY}{K}$ measures the amount by which the marginal product of capital is being reduced because of the accumulation of capital $\left(\dfrac{SY}{K}\right)$.

The relationship shown in equation (30) between $\dfrac{dy}{dt}$ and S (given the existing values of V, r_k, Y, K, and ϵ_k) is represented in Diagram VII.

Diagram VII

Since $\dfrac{dy}{dt} = S\dfrac{dV}{dt}$, $\dfrac{dy}{dt}$ will be zero when S is zero. The growth rate of the national income y (which equals $VS+r$) will in this case be constant at r. If now S is a small positive figure, $\dfrac{dV}{dt}$ will be positive since the tendency of invention to raise the marginal product of machinery (provided that r_k is positive) will outweigh the still very slight tendency for capital accumulation relatively to labour to cause the marginal product of machinery to fall. $\dfrac{dy}{dt}$

will have risen above zero if S is a small positive figure. But S might be so great that the rate of capital accumulation would be so high that the force of invention in raising the marginal product of machinery would be exactly outweighed by the force of capital accumulation in lowering the marginal product of machinery. $\dfrac{dV}{dt}$ would equal zero and so $\dfrac{dy}{dt}$ would once again be zero. The growth rate of the national income will once more be constant. Exactly halfway between these two points S will be at a level (i.e. $S = \dfrac{1}{2}\dfrac{K}{Y}\dfrac{r_k}{\epsilon_k}$) at which the growth rate of the national income will be increasing most rapidly. If S were greater than the value of $\dfrac{K}{Y}\dfrac{r_k}{\epsilon_k}$ then the effect of invention in raising the marginal product of machinery would be more than offset by the effect of capital accumulation in lowering the marginal product of machinery and $\dfrac{dV}{dt}$ would be negative. From this size of S onwards the growth rate of the national income will be falling $\left(\text{i.e. } \dfrac{dy}{dt} = S\dfrac{dV}{dt}\right.$ will be $< 0\Big)$.

(3) THE APPROACH TO THE STATE OF STEADY GROWTH

In the case in which U, Q, and r are constant we can integrate the relationship $y = Uk + Ql + r$ of equation (2) into the production function[1]

$$Y = RN^Z K^U L^Q \exp(rt)$$

where N^Z is a constant depending upon the constant supply of land N and R is the amount of output which would be produced by one unit of land, one unit of labour, and one unit of machinery in the state of technical knowledge existing at time o. If we assume that L grows at a constant rate l, we have $L = L_0 \exp(lt)$ and this production function becomes

$$Y = RN^Z L_0^Q K^U \exp([r + Ql]t). \qquad \ldots (31)$$

---

[1] In this function we write $\exp(rt)$ for e^{rt}. This form of expression for the exponential function is used throughout this book.

Since $Y_0 = RN^Z L_0^Q K_0^V$, we can write this

$$Y = Y_0 \left(\frac{K}{K_0}\right)^U \exp([r+Ql]t) \qquad \ldots (32)$$

Now we know that $k = \dfrac{SY}{K}$ or in other words that $\dfrac{dK}{dt}$ (the level of investment) is equal to SY (the level of saving). It follows that

$$\frac{dK}{dt} = SY_0 \left(\frac{K}{K_0}\right)^U \exp([r+Ql]t). \qquad \ldots (33)$$

If we integrate this equation, we obtain:

$$K = K_0 \left\{ \frac{SY_0}{K_0}\frac{1-U}{r+Ql} + \frac{1 - \dfrac{SY_0}{K_0}\dfrac{1-U}{r+Ql}}{\exp([r+Ql]t)} \right\}^{\frac{1}{1-U}} \exp\left(\frac{r+Ql}{1-U}t\right)$$

$$\ldots (34)$$

and by substituting this value for K into equation (32) we have:

$$Y = Y_0 \left\{ \frac{SY_0}{K_0}\frac{1-U}{r+Ql} + \frac{1 - \dfrac{SY_0}{K_0}\dfrac{1-U}{r+Ql}}{\exp([r+Ql]t)} \right\}^{\frac{U}{1-U}} \exp\left(\frac{r+Ql}{1-U}t\right).$$

$$\ldots (35)$$

Equations (34) and (35) give us the time paths of K and Y, starting from the initial values K_0 and Y_0. It should be observed that if we start with $\dfrac{SY_0}{K_0}$ (i.e. k_0) $= \dfrac{r+Ql}{1-U}$ then

$$\left.\begin{array}{l} K = K_0 \exp\left(\dfrac{r+Ql}{1-U}t\right) \\[3mm] Y = Y_0 \exp\left(\dfrac{r+Ql}{1-U}t\right) \end{array}\right\} \qquad \ldots (36)$$

and

As was shown on page 35 of the main text $\dfrac{r+Ql}{1-U}$ is the rate of steady growth; and it follows that if we start with K growing at this precise rate (i.e. with $k_0 = \dfrac{r+Ql}{1-U}$ then both K and Y will continue to grow at this same steady rate).

If now we divide both sides of equation (33) by K and then substitute for K on the right-hand side of equation (33) from equation (34) we obtain

$$k = \frac{\dfrac{r+Ql}{1-U}}{1 - \dfrac{k_0 - \dfrac{r+Ql}{1-U}}{k_0 \exp([r+Ql]t)}} \qquad \cdots (37)$$

where $k_0 = \dfrac{SY_0}{K_0}$. It will be observed from equation (37) that if $k_0 = \dfrac{r+Ql}{1-U}$, then $k = \dfrac{r+Ql}{1-U}$; that is to say, if we start with a rate of capital accumulation of $\dfrac{r+Ql}{1-U}$ we shall start and remain in a state of steady growth at this rate. It is further to be observed that as $t \to \infty$ so $k \to \dfrac{r+Ql}{1-U}$; that is to say, if we start with a rate of capital accumulation other than the steady-growth rate, we shall approach this rate of steady growth as time passes.

The time path of y can then be directly found by substituting the value of k from equation (37) into the expression for y in equation (2).

Moreover, since $\dfrac{SY}{K} = k$ we have $\dfrac{Y}{K} = \dfrac{k}{S}$, so that the time path of the income/capital ratio $\dfrac{Y}{K}$ can be deduced directly from equation (37) by multiplying the value of k by the constant $\dfrac{1}{S}$.

(4) THE LEVEL OF SAVINGS IN THE STATE OF STEADY GROWTH

We know from equation (37) that in the state of steady growth

$$k = \frac{SY}{K} = \frac{r+Ql}{1-U} \qquad \cdots (38)$$

and from this we see that

$$K = \frac{SY(1-U)}{r+Ql}. \qquad \ldots (39)$$

If we substitute this value of K in the production function (31) we get

$$Y = RN^Z L_0{}^Q \left\{ \frac{S(1-U)}{r+Ql} \right\}^U Y^U \exp([r+Ql]t)$$

or $\quad Y = R^{\frac{1}{1-U}} N^{\frac{Z}{1-U}} L_0{}^{\frac{Q}{1-U}} \left\{ \frac{S(1-U)}{r+Ql} \right\}^{\frac{U}{1-U}} \exp\left(\frac{r+Ql}{1-U}t\right) \ldots (40)$

which may be regarded as the basic form of expression of the production function in the state of steady growth.

If we differentiate this expression for Y partially in respect to S we obtain

$$\frac{S}{Y}\frac{\partial Y}{\partial S} = \frac{U}{1-U}. \qquad \ldots (41)$$

If we differentiate the expression for K and Y in equation (39) partially in respect of S, we obtain

$$\frac{S}{K}\frac{\partial K}{\partial S} = \frac{SY}{K}\frac{1-U}{r+Ql}\left(\frac{S}{Y}\frac{\partial Y}{\partial S} - 1\right).$$

If we then substitute into this expression the value of $\dfrac{SY}{K}$ from equation (38) and the value of $\dfrac{S}{Y}\dfrac{\partial Y}{\partial S}$ from equation (41) we obtain

$$\frac{S}{K}\frac{\partial K}{\partial S} = \frac{1}{1-U}. \qquad \ldots (42)$$

Now equation (38) tells us that, since in a state of steady growth $k = \dfrac{r+Ql}{1-U}$, the rate of capital accumulation and so the rate of growth of income will be unaffected by the level of the proportion of income saved in a state of steady growth. In the main text (pages 42 to 45) we discuss this apparent paradox at some length; and we conclude that while the *rate of growth* of capital and of income will be the same in two states of steady growth which differ only in the proportion of income saved, nevertheless the *absolute level* of the capital stock and of the national output will at each point of time be higher in that state of steady growth in which a higher proportion of income is saved. Equations (41) and (42) measure this effect of a higher S upon the absolute level of K and Y. Suppose that U were $\frac{1}{3}$. Then at each moment of time in a process of steady growth the national product would be $\frac{1}{2}$ per cent higher and the capital stock would be $1\frac{1}{2}$ per cent higher if the proportion of income had been persistently 1 per cent higher during this process of steady growth.

Equation (41) tells us that the higher the proportion of income saved the higher will be the level of income at each point of time in the process of steady growth. But it does not follow that the standard of living, i.e. the level of consumption, will necessarily be higher. Income is higher because savings are higher; but consumption is income minus savings; and the higher income may be offset by the higher savings so that consumption is lower.

Now $C = (1 - S)Y$, where C represents total consumption. Differentiating this we obtain

$$\frac{\partial C}{\partial S} = (1 - S)\frac{\partial Y}{\partial S} - Y$$

and substituting into this for $\dfrac{\partial Y}{\partial S}$ from equation (41) we obtain

$$\frac{S}{C}\frac{\partial C}{\partial S} = \frac{U - S}{(1 - S)(1 - U)}. \qquad \ldots (43)$$

It follows that a higher proportion of income saved will cause the level of consumption at each point of time in a process of steady growth to be higher, if $S < U$. But if the proportion of income saved S were higher than the proportion of income going to profits U, then a fall in the proportion of income saved would raise the level of consumption. The level of consumption will be maximised at each point of time if the proportion of income saved has been permanently set equal to the proportion of income going to profits.

The reader should not conclude from this that the optimum pattern for savings over time is to set $S = U$. Our analysis has been based on the assumption that S is to remain constant over time. We have been considering the effects on Y and C at each point of time of the choice between a higher or lower level for a constant S over time. If, for some unspecified reason, S must be held constant over time then $S = U$ is the constant level of S which will cause the standard of living to be at its highest at each point of time. But there is, of course, no reason to believe that the optimum time pattern of output and consumption will imply a constant level of S over time. It is a grave deficiency in this present book that it does not deal with the optimisation of savings and consumption over time; it merely examines the implications of different constant levels for savings as a ratio of different types of income (i.e. constant levels for S_w, S_v, and S_g).

(5) THE CASE OF OVERPOPULATION

Let us suppose that there is an indefinitely large supply of unemployed labour available for employment at a fixed 'subsistence' real wage rate W_s. Let us otherwise make the same assumptions as are made in this Appendix, i.e. three factors, land, labour, and machinery; one product; constant returns to scale; and perfect competition.

Since $Q = \dfrac{WL}{Y}$ and in our present case W is constant at W_s, we have

$$q = l - y \qquad \qquad \cdots (44)$$

where l now measures the growth rate of the employed population instead of the growth rate of the employable population. Let us suppose further that the elasticities of substitution between the three factors of production are all equal to each other at the value σ. Then by substituting into equation (44) for q from equation (17) and for y from equation (2) we have

$$l = \frac{U}{U+Z}k + \frac{\sigma}{U+Z}n. \qquad \cdots (45)$$

Substituting this value of l into equation (2) we have

$$y = \frac{U}{U+Z}k + \frac{\sigma Q}{U+Z}n + r. \qquad \ldots (46)$$

Equation (45) then expresses the proportionate rate at which the demand for labour for employment will grow at the constant real wage rate W_s; and this will depend upon the rates at which capital accumulation (k) and the process of technical improvement (r_l) are tending to raise the marginal product of labour. But the more important is land as a limiting factor of production (i.e. the smaller is $\frac{U}{U+Z}$), the less can employment expand without reducing again any rise in the real wage rate due to the accumulation of capital (k); and the more important are land and capital in production and the less easily labour can be substituted for land and capital (i.e. the smaller is $\frac{\sigma}{U+Z}$), the less can employment grow without offsetting any increase in the real wage rate above the subsistence level which had been caused by the process of technical innovation (r_l).

Equation (46) shows the rate at which the national income will be growing when capital is being accumulated at a rate $k\left(= \frac{SY}{K}\right)$ and when the amount of labour in employment is being increased continuously at that rate which is needed to prevent any rise in the real wage rate above the subsistence level W_s.

It is of interest to consider three special cases of equations (45) and (46).

(1) First, let us consider the case in which there are only two factors of production labour and machinery ($Z = 0$) and there is no technical progress ($r = r_l = 0$). Then from equations (45) and (46) we have $y = l = k$. Output, employment, and capital stock will all grow at the same rate. The reason for this is discussed in the main text (pages 49 and 50) where it is also shown that this growth of Y, L, and K will be at a constant steady-growth rate.

(2) Second, let us suppose that there are three factors of production, land, labour, and machinery ($Z > 0$) but that there is no technical progress ($r = r_l = 0$). We are concerned only with

movements along one unchanged production function with constant returns to scale. In this case equations (45) and (46) give $y = l = \dfrac{U}{U+Z}k$. This case is discussed on pages 50 and 51 of the main text. In this case l will be $< k$, because to maintain a given real wage rate labour must grow less rapidly than capital in order to offset the increased pressure upon the unchanged amount of land. y will also be less than k, because K will have increased in a larger ratio than either of the other two factors L or N which are used to produce Y. Since $y < k$, $\dfrac{Y}{K}$ and so $\dfrac{SY}{K}$ will be constantly falling. The rate of capital accumulation will be declining continuously.

(3) Third, let us suppose that there are only two factors, labour and machinery ($Z = 0$) but that technical progress takes place (r_l and $r \neq 0$). Then equations (45) and (46) give

$$l = k + \frac{\sigma}{U}r_l$$

and

$$y = k + \frac{\sigma Q}{U}r_l + r.$$

In this case $l > k$, because technical progress is tending to raise the marginal product of labour so that employment can grow more rapidly than the capital stock without any fall in the marginal product of labour and so in the real wage rate. y will also be $> k$ for two reasons: output will be growing faster than the capital stock, because the only other factor labour is itself growing more quickly than the capital stock; and in addition technical progress will be making output grow more quickly than the factors of production. Since $y > k$, $\dfrac{Y}{K}$ and so $\dfrac{SY}{K}$ will be constantly rising. The rate of capital accumulation will be continuously rising.

Let us next consider equations (45) and (46) on the assumptions that $\sigma = 1$ and $r_l = r$. These are the assumptions which must be made in order that the proportions of the national output going to the three factors (U, Q, and Z) should remain constant. We have seen in Chapter 4 and in Section (3) of this Appendix that when l is constant given independently by external demographic conditions, these assumptions lead eventually to a state of steady growth. We intend now to consider this problem on our present alternative assumption that l constantly adjusts itself to the level required to maintain W at the constant level W_s. With U, Q, and Z once again constant, shall we always approach a state of steady growth, when l is not a given constant but behaves in such a way as to keep the real wage rate constant?

With $\sigma = 1$ and $r_l = r$ equations (45) and (46) give

$$l = y = \frac{U}{U+Z}k + \frac{r}{U+Z}. \qquad \dots (47)$$

Now it is to be observed that this equation for y is of exactly the same form as

$$y = Uk + Ql + r \qquad \dots (2)$$

in the case examined in section (3). The only difference is that the constant U in equation (2) is replaced in (47) by the constant $\frac{U}{U+Z}$ and the constant $Ql+r$ in (2) is replaced by the constant $\frac{r}{U+Z}$ in (47). We can, therefore, go through the whole analysis of Section (3) with these substitutions.

Thus we now start with the production function,

$$Y = Y_0\left(\frac{K}{K_0}\right)^{\frac{U}{U+Z}} \exp\left(\frac{r}{U+Z}t\right) \qquad \dots (48)$$

which replaces equation (32).

Remembering that $\frac{dK}{dt} = SY$ we can then replace equation (33) with

$$\frac{dK}{dt} = SY_0\left(\frac{K}{K_0}\right)^{\frac{U}{U+Z}} \exp\left(\frac{r}{U+Z}t\right) \qquad \dots (49)$$

and obtain by integration, instead of equations (34) and (35), the following results:

$$K = K_0 \left\{ \frac{SY_0}{K_0} \frac{Z}{r} + \frac{1 - \dfrac{SY_0}{K_0} \dfrac{Z}{r}}{\exp\left(\dfrac{r}{U+Z}t\right)} \right\}^{\frac{U+Z}{Z}} \exp\left(\frac{r}{Z}t\right) \quad \ldots (50)$$

and

$$Y = Y_0 \left\{ \frac{SY_0}{K_0} \frac{Z}{r} + \frac{1 - \dfrac{SY_0}{K_0} \dfrac{Z}{r}}{\exp\left(\dfrac{r}{U+r}t\right)} \right\}^{\frac{U}{Z}} \exp\left(\frac{r}{Z}t\right) \quad \ldots (51)$$

From (47) we know that in the present case $l = y$. It follows that $\dfrac{Y}{L}$ is constant at $\dfrac{L_0}{Y_0}$, so that $L = \dfrac{L_0}{Y_0} Y$, so that the value of L, the volume of employment, is given also by equation (51).

In the main text, it is shown that in the circumstances now under discussion there is a steady growth rate $\dfrac{r}{Z}$ towards which the economy will tend. If we assume that $k_0 \left(\equiv \dfrac{SY}{K_0} \right) = \dfrac{r}{Z}$, i.e. that the initial rate of growth was this steady-growth rate then we have from equations (50) and (51)

and
$$\left. \begin{array}{c} K = K_0 \exp\left(\dfrac{r}{Z}t\right) \\[2mm] Y = Y_0 \exp\left(\dfrac{r}{Z}t\right) \end{array} \right\} \quad \ldots (52)$$

That is to say both K and Y continue to grow at this steady-growth rate $\dfrac{r}{Z}$.

If we divide both sides of (49) by K and then substitute for

K on the right-hand side of (49) from (50) we obtain:

$$k = \frac{\dfrac{r}{Z}}{1 - \dfrac{k_0 - \dfrac{r}{Z}}{k_0 \exp\left(\dfrac{r}{U+Z}t\right)}} \qquad \ldots (53)$$

which replaces equation (37). Once again as $t \to \infty$, so $k \to$ the steady-growth rate $\dfrac{r}{Z}$.

The time path of y and l can then be found by substituting for k from equation (53) into equation (47).

By means of equation (53) we can now discuss the three special cases in which (i) $r = 0$ but $Z \neq 0$, (2) $r \neq 0$ but $Z = 0$, and (3) $r = Z = 0$.

(1) This is the case of movement along a given production function, but with Q and U constant because of our assumptions that $\sigma = 1$ and $r_l = r$. From (53) we have

$$k = \frac{k_0 \exp\left(\dfrac{r}{U+Z}t\right)}{1 + k_0 \dfrac{Z}{U+Z}\left\{\dfrac{\exp\left[\dfrac{r}{U+Z}t\right] - 1}{\dfrac{r}{U+Z}}\right\}}.$$

If $r \to 0$, $\dfrac{r}{V+Z}$ also $\to 0$. And in the above expression for k, as $\dfrac{r}{U+Z} \to 0$,

$$k \to \frac{k_0}{1 + k_0 \dfrac{Z}{U+Z}t}.$$

We have, therefore, in this case

$$k\left(\equiv \frac{1}{K}\frac{dK}{dt}\right) = \frac{k_0}{\left|1 + k_0\dfrac{Z}{U+Z}t\right.} . \qquad \ldots (54)$$

This gives the rate of capital accumulation which falls steadily towards zero as time passes. The growth rate of output and of employment can be obtained from (54) and from (47) with $r = 0$ as

$$y = l = \frac{U}{U+Z}\frac{k_0}{1 + k_0\dfrac{Z}{U+Z}t}$$

which also fall continually over time.

By integration of (54) we can obtain:

$$K = K_0\left(1 + k_0\frac{Z}{U+Z}t\right)^{\left(1+\frac{U}{Z}\right)} \qquad \ldots (55)$$

Substituting this value of K into (48) with $r = 0$ we obtain:

$$Y = Y_0\left(1 + k_0\frac{Z}{U+Z}t\right). \qquad \ldots (56)$$

Equation (56) shows that in this case Y increases at a constant linear (instead of proportionate) rate. Each year Y is larger by the same absolute amount, namely $Y_0\dfrac{k_0 Z}{U+Z}$.

(2) In this case we assume $Z = 0$ but $r \neq 0$. We now obtain from equation (53):

$$k\left(\equiv \frac{1}{K}\frac{dK}{dt}\right) = k_0\exp\left(\frac{r}{U}t\right). \qquad \ldots (57)$$

From equation (57) and from equation (47) with $Z = 0$ we have

$$l = y = k_0\exp\left(\frac{r}{U}t\right) + \frac{r}{U}.$$

This is a highly explosive situation. The rate of capital accumulation itself grows at the constant proportionate growth rate of

$\dfrac{r}{U}$ and the growth rate of output and employment is equal to the proportionate growth rate $\dfrac{r}{U}$ plus a growth rate which is itself growing at the growth rate $\dfrac{r}{U}$.

By integration of (57) we obtain

$$K = K_0 \exp\left\{\frac{Uk_0}{r}\left(\exp\left[\frac{r}{U}t\right] - 1\right)\right\} \qquad \ldots (58)$$

and substituting this value of K into (48) with $Z = 0$ we have

$$Y = Y_0 \exp\left\{\frac{Uk_0}{r}\left(\exp\left[\frac{r}{U}\right] - 1\right) + \frac{r}{U}t\right\} \qquad \ldots (59)$$

These two equations give the explosive time paths of K and Y.

(3) Assume now that $Z = r = 0$. We are dealing with a constant-returns production function with no limiting third factor land and with no technical progress. Equation (57) gives the value of k with $Z = 0$. If we write $r = 0$ in equation (57) we get

$$k\left(\equiv \frac{1}{K}\frac{dK}{dt}\right) = k_0. \qquad \ldots (60)$$

By integration we have

$$K = K_0 \exp(k_0 t). \qquad \ldots (61)$$

Substituting this value of K into (48) with $Z = r = 0$, we have

$$Y = Y_0 \exp(k_0 t). \qquad \ldots (62)$$

In other words Y and K both grow at the constant growth rate k_0. We are back at a special case of the special case (1) discussed on page 50 above. We there showed that with any constant-returns production function with only two factors of production, labour and machinery, and with no technical progress, Y, K, and L would all grow at a constant steady growth-rate equal to

$\frac{SY_0}{K_0}(\equiv k_0)$. We are dealing in equations (60) to (62) with the same situation together with the additional (and unnecessary) assumption that $\sigma = 1$. In fact U and Q $(= 1 - U)$ remain constant because $\frac{K}{L}$ remains constant; there is no need to make the additional assumption that $\sigma = 1$ in order to achieve this result.

A Two-Product Economy

(1) INTRODUCTION

The purpose of this Appendix is to work out in some detail the changing relationships through time in a growing economy in which there are two distinct industries, producing capital goods and consumption goods. That is to say, we examine in this Appendix the effects of dropping the assumption of 'perfect substitutability in production between capital goods and consumption goods', (See page 6 above). We no longer assume that technical progress is the same in the two industries or that the factor-intensities and elasticities of substitution between the factors are necessarily the same in the two industries. The cost price of capital goods may thus move in a different way from the cost price of consumption goods. Otherwise throughout this Appendix we make essentially all the same assumptions as those made in Chapter I of the main text.

But in Section (2) of this Appendix we assume that there are only two factors of production (labour and machinery) instead of three (land, labour, and machinery). With this extra simplifying assumption we are able to consider the relationships which must exist at any one moment of time between the growth rates of the various quantities in our economic system.

In Section (3) we drop the simplifying assumption that there are only two factors of production and introduce once more the third factor, land. But we now introduce simplifying assumptions of a kind that keep the distribution of income between the three factors unchanged. On this basis we are able to go a great deal further than in Section (2) of this Appendix in examining for our two-industry economy, not only the relationships which must exist at any given moment of time between the growth rates of the different variables in our economy, but also the actual path through time of each of the main variables.

(2) TWO FACTORS WITH A VARIABLE DISTRIBUTION OF INCOME

Consider an economy described by the eleven equations (2.1) to (2.11):

$$K = K_m + K_c \qquad \ldots (2.1)$$

$$L = L_m + L_c \qquad \ldots (2.2)$$

$$M = M(L_m, K_m, t) \qquad \ldots (2.3)$$

$$C = C(L_c, K_c, t) \qquad \ldots (2.4)$$

The total stock of machinery in the economy at any one moment of time (K) is equal to the amount used in the capital-goods industry (K_m) plus the amount used in the consumption-goods industry (K_c). Similarly, the total amount of labour (L) is used either in the capital-goods industry (L_m) or in the consumption-goods industry (L_c). The current output of capital goods (M) is a function of the amounts of the two factors employed in the production of M (namely, L_m and K_m) and, since technical progress is continuously raising the productivity of the factors, also of the date or time (t) at which production is taking place. There is a similar production function for the current output of consumption goods (C).

For equations (2.1) to (2.4) we have a choice of defining M either (i) as the gross output of capital goods including both those which are necessary to meet the depreciation of the existing stock of machines and those which are added to the stock of machines or (ii) as the net output of capital goods available for addition to the stocks of machines after deduction of the output of capital goods required to meet the depreciation of the existing stock of machines. If we adopt (i), then L_c and K_c included only the labour and machines which are used directly to produce consumption goods, but L_m and K_m include all the labour and machines used to produce capital goods, including the capital goods purchased by the industry producing consumption goods for the maintenance of its stock of machines. If we adopt (ii), we must interpret the production function of consumption goods—namely, $C = C(L_c, K_c, t)$ —differently. We must take C to represent the maximum amount of consumption goods that could be produced with an amount of labour L_c and an amount of machinery K_c, if L_c and K_c were responsible not only for producing C but also for producing the capital goods necessary to meet the depreciation of K_c. Or, to put it the other way round, we must take L_c and K_c to represent the amounts of labour and machinery which would be necessary to produce an output of consumption goods C plus an output of capital goods sufficient to meet the depreciation on K_c. If we adopt (ii), then L_m and K_m are the amounts of labour and machinery which are required to produce an amount of capital goods equal to M plus the amount of capital goods needed to meet the depreciation on the capital stock K_m. M is then the output of capital goods available for net investment to add to the stock of machines.

Both these definitions have their advantages and their dis-advantages. There would be two main advantages in adopting definition (i). First, we shall in what follows discuss the effects of differences in the technical conditions of production in the two industries, and it is certainly more natural to treat the whole industry producing capital goods (including that part which produces capital goods for the replacement of the machines used in the industry producing consumption goods) as a homogeneous industry than it is to include part of it, as it were, inside the industry producing consumption goods. Second, the choice of definition (i) would make it possible to develop our model so as to consider problems arising from depreciation by sudden death as well as those arising from depreciation by evaporation. If we use definition (ii) we must assume depreciation by evaporation. To be able to use definition (ii) the need for capital goods to meet the depreciation of K_c must be strictly related to the size of K_c and not to the age distribution of K_c. If in fact machines needed to be replaced if they were old but not if they were young, then with a given L_c and K_c C would be high if the capital instruments K_c were young (so that not much of the L_c and K_c was needed to maintain the K_c) but would be low if the machines K_c were old (so that much of the L_c and K_c was needed to replace the K_c). There would no longer with definition (ii) be a unique relationship between C on the one hand and L_c and K_c on the other.

On the other hand, the use of definition (ii) has two great advantages. First, if definition (i) is adopted, we would in Section (3) of this Appendix have to make the unnatural assumption that a constant proportion of gross profits (i.e. profits before deduction of depreciation allowances) was always saved; for this assumption would in this case be necessary to give the 'constant-proportions' conditions required for the analysis in Section (3). With definition (ii) it is possible to make the much more natural assumption that a constant proportion of net profits (after setting aside depreciation allowances) is saved. Second, the adoption of definition (ii) makes possible an immense simplification of the algebra in this Appendix without the sacrifice of the main points which it is designed to illustrate. It has, therefore, been decided to adopt definition (ii)[1].

Let us return to the exposition of the basic relationships in our economy.

$$W = C_l \qquad \qquad \ldots (2.5)$$

$$W = PM_l \qquad \qquad \ldots (2.6)$$

The wage-rate (W) measured in terms of money or of consumption goods (since we are assuming the money price of consumption goods to be constant) is in both industries equal to the value of the marginal product of labour. In the consumption-goods industry this is equal to $\dfrac{\partial C}{\partial L_c}$ which we write as C_l. In the capital-goods industry the marginal product of labour in terms of capital goods equals $\dfrac{\partial M}{\partial L_m}$ or M_l, and in terms of money or of consumption goods this equals PM_l, where P is the price of capital goods in terms of money or of consumption goods.

$$PV = C_k \qquad \qquad \ldots (2.7)$$

$$V = M_k \qquad \qquad \ldots (2.8)$$

In equilibrium the profit earned on a machine will also be equal to the value of the marginal product of that machine. If V

---

[1] I must thank Mr D. G. Champernowne for pointing out to me the possibility and great advantages of adopting definition (ii). I have done so with some reluctance because I had worked the whole Appendix in terms of definition (i) which enabled me to end the Appendix with some discussion of the implications of replacing the assumption of depreciation by sudden death for the assumption of depreciation by evaporation, and thereby to show that in the 'constant-proportions' case there would be a steady-growth state in the case of depreciation by sudden death as well as in the case of depreciation by evaporation. But on balance, I think, the gain outweighs any loss in adopting definition (ii).

is the net rate of profit (i.e. the rate of profit after deduction of depreciation allowance) then PV is the amount of net profit per machine; and this must be equal to the value of the net marginal product of a machine. In the consumption-goods industry, the marginal net product—and the value of the marginal net product —of a machine is $\dfrac{\partial C}{\partial K_c}$ or C_k. In the capital-goods industry the marginal net product of a machine is $\dfrac{\partial M}{\partial K_m}$ or M_k, so that the value of the marginal product is PM_k. Since $PV = PM_k$, we have $V = M_k$. Thus the net rate of profit in our economy is equal to the marginal net product of machines in the capital-goods industry.

$$MP = SY \qquad \qquad \dots (2.9)$$

S is the proportion of the net national income (Y) which is saved and used for net investment, i.e. for a net addition to the stock of machines. But net investment must be equal to the value of the output of capital goods (MP).

$$Y = MP + C \; (= WL + PVK) \qquad \dots (2.10)$$

The net national income (Y) is equal to net investment (MP) plus consumption (C). It is also equal to the total wage bill (WL) plus the total of net profits (PVK). But these two equations are not independent. Since we are assuming constant returns to scale the output of each industry will be just sufficient to pay each factor a reward equal to the value of its marginal net product, or

$$C = L_c C_l + K_c C_k = WL_c + PVK_c$$

and

$$M = L_m M_l + K_m M_k = \frac{W}{P} L_m + VK_m.$$

Therefore

$$MP + C = WL + PVK.$$

$$Q = \frac{WL}{Y}. \qquad \qquad \dots (2.11)$$

Q is an expression for the proportion of the net national income which goes to wages.

Equations (2.9) and (2.10) have in fact introduced a simple element of social accounting into our system. It will be useful to

expand this a little for future use. Consider the following relationships:

$$
\left.
\begin{array}{ccc}
WL_m + WL_c & = & WL \\
+ \quad\quad + & & + \\
PVK_m + PVK_c & = & PVK \\
= \quad\quad = & & = \\
MP + \quad C & = & Y
\end{array}
\right\} . \qquad \ldots (2.12)
$$

The first row in (2.12) expresses the fact that the wage bill in the
capital-goods industry (WL_m) plus the wage bill in the consumption-goods industry (WL_c) equals the total wage bill (WL); and
similarly the second row divides total profits between the two
industries. The first column expresses the fact that the value of
the output of capital goods (MP) is equal to the wage bill plus tne
profits made in this industry; and the second column expresses
the similar relationships in the consumption-good industry. Thus
the sum of the four elements WL_m, WL_c, PVK_m, and PVK_c makes
up the total national income (Y), which can be expressed either
as $MP+C$ or as $WL+PVK$.

For convenience in expressing our results in what follows we
can write each of the elements in (2.12) as proportions of the
national income. This is done in (2.13).

$$
\left.
\begin{array}{ccc}
Q_m S + Q_c(1-S) & = & Q \\
+ \quad\quad\quad + & & + \\
(1-Q_m)S + (1-Q_c)(1-S) & = & 1-Q \\
= \quad\quad\quad\quad = & & = \\
S \quad + \quad 1-S & = & 1
\end{array}
\right\} . \qquad \ldots (2.13)
$$

In (2.13) Q_m is the proportion of the value of the output of capital
goods which goes in wages in that industry; and since the value
of the output of capital goods is a proportion S of the national
income, $Q_m S$ is the wage bill in the capital goods industry
expressed as a proportion of the national income. Similarly, Q_c
is the proportion of the value of the output of consumption goods
which goes to wages in that industry. Q is the proportion of the
total national income which goes to wages. We can use the
information in (2.13) to express various structural relationships in
our economy in terms of the four proportions Q_c, Q_m, Q, and S.

For example,

$$\frac{K_c}{K} = \frac{K_c PV}{KPV} = \frac{(1 - Q_c)(1 - S)}{1 - Q}.$$

Moreover, since $Q = Q_m S + Q_c(1 - S)$ from row 1 of (2.13), we have in fact only three and not four independent proportions. We can from this equation express any one of these four proportions in terms of the other three. We shall make use of these relationships in deriving a number of the expressions which follow.

We may now differentiate the eleven equations (2.1) to (2.11) in respect to time in order to consider the rate of growth of the different variables in our economy. We will adopt the following notation. The capital letters used in equations (2.1) to (2.11) above all represent the absolute value of some variable in our economy at any given point of time. Thus K = the stock of machinery existing at a given moment of time, M = the rate of output of capital goods at a given moment of time, and S = the proportion of the national income saved at a given moment of time. We will use the corresponding small letters to represent the proportionate rates of change of these variables at any moment of time. Thus

$$k = \frac{1}{K} \frac{dK}{dt}, \quad m = \frac{1}{M} \frac{dM}{dt}, \quad s = \frac{1}{S} \frac{dS}{dt},$$

and so on for all the other original variables.

If we differentiate our eleven equations (2.1) to (2.11), using this notation, we obtain from equations (2.1) and (2.2):

$$k = \frac{(1 - Q_m)S}{1 - Q} k_m + \frac{(1 - Q_c)(1 - S)}{1 - Q} k_c \qquad \ldots (2.14)$$

$$l = \frac{Q_m S}{Q} l_m + \frac{Q_c(1 - S)}{Q} l_c. \qquad \ldots (2.15)$$

From equation (2.3):

$$m = Q_m l_m + (1 - Q_m)k_m + r_m \qquad \ldots (2.16)$$

where $r_m = \dfrac{1}{M} \dfrac{\partial M}{\partial t}$ or the rate of technical progress in the capital-goods industry, i.e. the rate at which the output of that industry would grow if the factors employed in it remained constant but the mere passage of time brought consequential improvements of technical methods as knowledge increased.

From equation (2.4):

$$c = Q_c l_c + (1 - Q_c)k_c + r_c \qquad \ldots (2.17)$$

where r_c is the rate of technical progress in the consumption-goods industry.

From equation (2.5):

$$w = \frac{L_c}{W}C_{ll}l_c + \frac{K_c}{W}C_{lk}k_c + r_{lc} \qquad \ldots (2.18')$$

where

$$C_{ll} = \frac{\partial C_l}{\partial L}, \quad C_{lk} = \frac{\partial C_l}{\partial K_c}, \quad \text{and } r_{lc} = \frac{1}{C_l}\frac{\partial C_l}{\partial t}.$$

r_{lc} is thus the rate at which the marginal product of labour in the consumption-goods industry is rising as a result of technical progress.

Similarly, from equations (2.6), (2.7), and (2.8):

$$w - p = \frac{PL_m}{W}M_{ll}l_m + \frac{PK_m}{W}M_{lk}k_m + r_{lm} \qquad \ldots (2.19')$$

$$v + p = \frac{L_c}{PV}C_{kl}l_c + \frac{K_c}{P_v}C_{kk}k_c + r_{kc} \qquad \ldots (2.20')$$

$$v = \frac{L_m}{V}M_{kl}l_m + \frac{K_m}{V}M_{kk}k_m + r_{km} \qquad \ldots (2.21')$$

where

$$M_{ll} = \frac{\partial M_l}{\partial L_m}, \quad M_{lk} = \frac{\partial M_l}{\partial K_m} \quad \text{and } r_{lm} = \frac{1}{M_l}\frac{\partial M_l}{\partial t}$$

and similarly for the corresponding terms in equations (2.20') and (2.21').

From equations (2.9) and (2.10):

$$m + p = s + y \qquad \ldots (2.22)$$

$$\left. \begin{aligned} y &= S(m+p) + (1 - S)c \\ &= Q(w+l) + (1-Q)(p+v+k) \end{aligned} \right\} \qquad \ldots (2.23)$$

From equation (2.11):

$$q = w + l - y. \qquad \ldots (2.24)$$

The eleven equations (2.14) to (2.24) express the relationships between the rates of growth and rates of change of the variables in our economy. We can, however, greatly simplify equations (2.18'), (2.19'), (2.20'), and (2.21') as a result of our assumption that there are constant returns to scale in both industries, by expressing the terms C_{ll}, C_{lk}, M_{ll}, M_{lk}, etc. in terms of the elasticities of substitution between labour and machinery as factors of production in the two industries.

Consider any production function

$$X = X(K, L)$$

where X is the output of a product produced by two factors K and L. If there are constant returns to scale, then

$$X = X_k K + X_l L$$

since the function X is in this case homogeneous of the first degree. If now we differentiate these two expressions for X, we obtain respectively

$$dX = X_k \, dK + X_l \, dL$$

and

$$dX = (X_k + K X_{kk} + L X_{lk}) \, dK + (X_l + K X_{kl} + LK_{ll}) \, dL$$

Both these expressions for dX are true for all values of dK and dL. If we take the difference between these two equations for dX we have

$$0 = dK(K X_{kk} + L X_{lk}) + dL(K X_{kl} + L X_{ll})$$

which must also be valid for all values of dK and dL. It follows that

$$K X_{kk} + L X_{lk} = 0$$

and

$$K X_{kl} + L X_{ll} = 0$$

where, as is true of all continuous functions, $X_{lk} = X_{kl}$.

Applying these conclusions to our two industries we have:

$$C_{ll} = -\frac{K_c}{L_c}C_{lk}, \qquad M_{ll} = -\frac{K_m}{L_m}M_{lk},$$

$$C_{kl} = C_{lk}, \qquad M_{kl} = M_{lk}, \qquad \left.\begin{array}{c} \\ \\ \\ \end{array}\right\} \ \dots \ (2.25)$$

$$C_{kk} = -\frac{L_c}{K_c}C_{lk}, \qquad M_{kk} = -\frac{L_m}{K_m}M_{lk}$$

By means of the expressions in (2.25) we can eliminate C_{ll}, C_{kl}, C_{kk}, M_{ll}, M_{kl}, and M_{kk} from equations (2.18'), (2.19'), (2.20'), and (2.21'). We are left with the terms C_{lk} and M_{lk} in these four equations. But we can express C_{lk} in terms of σ_c, the elasticity of substitution between K_c and L_c in the production of C; and similarly we can express M_{lk} in terms of σ_m.

For this purpose consider again the constant-returns production function $X = X(K, L)$. We define the elasticity of substitution (σ) between L and K in the production of X as the percentage increase in the ratio of L to K which will be used in the production of X as a result of a 1 per cent fall in the price (i.e. the marginal product) of L relatively to the price (i.e. the marginal product) of K, or

$$\sigma = -\frac{(dL/L)-(dK/K)}{\dfrac{dX_l}{X_l}-\dfrac{dX_k}{X_k}}$$

$$= -\frac{(dL/L)-(dK/K)}{\dfrac{X_{ll}dL + X_{lk}dK}{X_l} - \dfrac{X_{kl}dL + X_{kk}dK}{X_k}}$$

But since $X_{kl} = X_{lk}$, $X_{ll} = -\dfrac{K}{L}X_{lk}$, and $X_{kk} = -\dfrac{L}{K}X_{lk}$ we have

$$\sigma = \frac{X_l X_k}{X_k K + X_l L}\frac{1}{X_{lk}}$$

or

$$X_{lk} = \frac{X_l X_k}{X}\frac{1}{\sigma}.$$

Similarly,

$$C_{lk} = \frac{WPV}{C}\frac{1}{\sigma_c} \quad \text{and} \quad M_{lk} = \frac{WV}{MP}\frac{1}{\sigma_m}$$

If we make these substitutions in equations (2.18'), (2.19'), (2.20') and (2.21'), we obtain

$$w = \frac{1-Q_c}{\sigma_c}(k_c - l_c) + r_{lc} \qquad \ldots (2.18)$$

$$w-p = \frac{1-Q_m}{\sigma_m}(k_m - l_m) + r_{lm} \qquad \ldots (2.19)$$

$$v+p = -\frac{Q_c}{\sigma_c}(k_c - l_c) + r_{kc} \qquad \ldots (2.20)$$

$$v = \frac{Q_m}{\sigma_m}(k_m - l_m) + r_{km}. \qquad \ldots (2.21)$$

The eleven equations ((2.14) to (2.24)) give us a set of relationships between 20 rates of growth (k_m, k_c, l_m, l_c, m, c, w, p, v, y, q, k, l, s, r_m, r_c, r_{lc}, r_{lm}, r_{kc}, and r_{km}) in terms of various structural parameters of the system. We can, therefore, express any one of the first eleven of these rates of growth in terms of k, l, s, and the six r's and of the structural parameters of the system. l (the rate of population growth) and the six r's (various measures of the rate of technical progress) are all taken as given by outside forces. k (the rate of capital accumulation) and s (the rate at which the ratio of savings to income is rising or falling) both depend upon the thriftiness conditions within the economic system. These thriftiness conditions we have not yet introduced: equation (2.9) merely defines S as the ratio of savings to income, it does not say what determines the value of S. We shall introduce an equation expressing the thriftiness conditions in due course; for the moment we take k and s as being determined by some unspecified forces.

At this stage we will make use of our eleven equations to find the value of $w-p-v$ in terms of k, l, s, and the six r's. We will write $w-p-v$ as μ. It measures the proportionate change in $\frac{W}{PV}$ i.e. the proportionate change in the ratio between the wage earned by a unit of labour and the profit earned on a machine.

In a competitive economy this measures the proportionate change in the ratio between the cost of hiring one more unit of labour and the cost of using one more machine. As we shall see, this term plays a most important role in our system.

From our eleven equations we obtain:

$$\mu(\equiv w - p - v) = \frac{k - l + \overline{\sigma\beta}\left(1 - \lambda^2 \dfrac{S_1 \overline{- S}}{Q_1 \overline{- Q}}\right) - s\lambda \dfrac{S}{Q_1 \overline{- Q}}}{1 + (\bar{\sigma} - 1)\left(1 - \lambda^2 \dfrac{S_1 \overline{- S}}{Q_1 \overline{- Q}}\right)}. \quad (2.26)$$

We must pause to explain and comment on some of the terms in equation (2.26). $\lambda = Q_c - Q_m$ and measures the difference between the labour-intensity of production in the consumption-goods industry and the capital-goods industry. $\bar{\sigma}$ is a weighted average of the two elasticities of substitution σ_c and σ_m, these being weighted by the terms $(1 - S)Q_c(1 - Q_c)$ and $S \cdot Q_m(1 - Q_m)$ respectively. It can be shown by means of the social-accounting relationships of (2.13) that

$$(1 - S)Q_c(1 - Q_c) + SQ_m(1 - Q_m) = Q(1 - Q) - \lambda^2 S(1 - S).$$

It follows, therefore, that

$$1 - \lambda^2 \frac{S_1 \overline{- S}}{Q_1 \overline{- Q}}$$

in equation (2.26) is a positive fraction lying between 0 and 1.

The term $\overline{\sigma\beta}$ depends upon the extent to which technical progress is biassed in the direction of labour-saving or of capital-saving inventions in the capital-goods industry and the consumption-goods industry. In order to understand this term it is necessary to consider certain relationships between the six r's which we have used in our basic equations to describe the amount and the form of technical progress. In fact with our constant-returns production function there are only four and not six, independent measures of technical progress: for r_c, the rate of technical progress in the consumption-goods industry can be expressed in terms of r_{lc} and r_{kc}, the rates at which the marginal products of labour and of machinery are being raised by technical progress in the consumption-goods industry; and similarly r_m can be expressed in terms of r_{lm} and r_{lk}. Since there are constant returns in the consumption-goods industry, we have:

$$C = C_l L_c + C_k K_c.$$

Keeping L_c and K_c constant and allowing only the passage of time and so technical progress to change C, we have:

$$\frac{\text{I}}{C}\frac{\partial C}{\partial t} = \frac{C_l L_c}{C}\frac{\text{I}}{C_l}\frac{\partial C_l}{\partial t} + \frac{C_k K_c}{C}\frac{\text{I}}{C_k}\frac{\partial C_k}{\partial t}$$

or

$$\left.\begin{aligned} r_c &= Q_c r_{lc} + (\text{I} - Q_c) r_{kc} \\[2mm] r_m &= Q_m r_{lm} + (\text{I} - Q_m) r_{km} \end{aligned}\right\} \qquad \dots (2.27)$$

and similarly

Now the form of our eleven equations is such that when we use them to evaluate the various rates of growth in the economy r_{lc} and r_{kc} always appear either (i) in the form of $Q_c r_{lc} + (\text{I} - Q_c) r_{kc}$ or (ii) in the form of $r_{lc} - r_{kc}$. The expression (i) is, as we have just seen, equal to r_c, the rate of technical progress in the consumption-goods industry. The expression (ii) is the excess of the rate of growth of the marginal product of labour over the rate of growth of the marginal product of machinery resulting from technical progress in the consumption-goods industry. Let us write β_{lc} for $r_{lc} - r_c$ (i.e. the measure of labour-saving bias in the consumption-goods industry) and, similarly, β_{kc} for $r_{kc} - r_c$. We can then write $\beta_c = \beta_{lc} - \beta_{kc} = r_{lc} - r_{kc}$ for the measure of the bias of technical progress in the consumption-goods industry in the direction of labour-using or machinery-saving; for if technical progress raises the marginal product of labour more rapidly than the marginal product of machinery there will, at any given cost of using a unit of labour (W) and cost of using a machine (PV), be an incentive to use a higher ratio of labour to machinery in production. Similarly we shall write $r_{lm} - r_{km}$ as β_m, the measure of the labour-using or machinery-saving nature of technical progress in the capital-goods industry. $\overline{\sigma\beta}$ in equation (2.26) is the weighted average of $\sigma_c \beta_c$ and $\sigma_m \beta_m$, the weights being once more $(\text{I} - S) \cdot Q_c (\text{I} - Q_c)$ and $S \cdot Q_m (\text{I} - Q_m)$ respectively. It is in this form that any bias in technical progress in fact enters into our system of equations.

It is important to observe that there are two quite distinct and separate forms of bias in technical progress in our system. The first may be expressed by $r_c - r_m$ and measures the extent to which technical progress is taking place more rapidly in the consumption-goods industries than in the capital-goods industries and so, as we shall see, tending to raise the price of capital goods in terms of consumption goods. The second is expressed by $\overline{\sigma\beta}$, i.e. by some average of $r_{lc} - r_{kc}$ and of $r_{lm} - r_{km}$ and measures the extent to which throughout the economy technical progress is raising the marginal productivity of labour more rapidly than that of capital instruments and so, as we shall see, tending to raise the wages per worker relatively to profits per machine. These two types of bias in technical progress are quite independent of each other in the sense that a given amount of technical progress can have any degree of either of these two biasses. But the two biasses have, of course, many repercussions and interrelationships in the final determination of the rates of growth of the different variables in our system. It is one of the objects of our model to elucidate these interrelationships.

If we now consider equation (2.26), we can see that there are three main factors which will tend to raise μ, i.e. to cause a rapid rate of rise in the ratio of wages per worker to profits per machine.

First, a high level of $k - l$ will have this effect. If the stock of machinery is growing more rapidly than the working population, then machines must be used in a higher ratio to labour throughout industry; and in order to induce producers so to change their techniques of production, the cost of a unit of labour must rise relatively to the cost of employing another machine. As would be expected, the rise in the price of labour relatively to that of employing another machine would be smaller, the larger is the elasticity of substitution between the two factors; for in this case a smaller change in relative prices is sufficient to give producers an incentive to make a large change in the labour-intensity of their production techniques; and we see from equation (2.26) that $k - l$ will have a smaller influence on μ, the larger is $\bar{\sigma}$.

Second, high values of β_c and β_m and so of $\overline{\sigma\beta}$ will give a high value of μ. The reason for this is obvious. If technical progress tends to raise the marginal product of labour relatively to the marginal product of a machine, then W must tend to rise relatively to PV to maintain equilibrium in a competitive economy in which factors are paid rewards equal to the value of their marginal products.

Thirdly, a high level of s will lead to a high level of μ if λ is < 0, i.e. if $Q_c < Q_m$. A high level of s means that as time passes the proportion of income saved is, for some reason or another, rising. This means that there is a corresponding shift of total demand away from consumption goods on to capital goods. But if capital goods are more labour-intensive than consumption goods in their production ($Q_m > Q_c$), this means a shift of demand away from the production of goods which require an unusually high ratio of machinery in their production on to goods which require an abnormally high ratio of labour in their production. This represents an indirect shift of demand away from the use of machines on to labour and thus tends to raise the ratio of W to PV.

Let us next introduce the thriftiness conditions into our system of equations. We have to express k and s in terms of the factors determining the propensity to save in our economy. As far as k is concerned, this is simple. The proportionate rate of growth in the stock of capital instruments is equal to the value of net investment divided by the value of the existing capital stock. In other words, in what follows we could write:

$$k = \frac{SY}{PK}. \qquad \qquad \ldots (2.28)$$

Thus the rate of accumulation of machinery equals the ratio of income to the value of the capital stock $\left(\frac{Y}{KP}\right)$ multiplied by the proportion of income which is saved (S). In this model we shall not carry this matter further. But its further development is an essential feature of the model developed in Section (3) below.

While k depends upon the absolute level of the proportion of income which is saved, s depends upon the rate at which this proportion is rising or falling. This in turn depends upon what is happening over time to the distribution of income between wages and profits and upon any difference in the propensity to save out of wages and out of profits. If S_w and S_v are the proportions of wages and net profits respectively which are not spent on consumption goods, we have

$$SY = S_w WL + S_v PVK. \qquad \ldots (2.29)$$

We shall assume that both S_w and S_v are constant.

By differentiation of (2.29) and the use of (2.23) we have:

$$s = -\frac{\gamma}{S}Q(1-Q)(\mu-k+l) \qquad \ldots (2.30)$$

where $\gamma = S_v - S_w$ or the excess of the proportion of profits over the proportion of wages which are saved. Substituting this value of s into (2.26) we have:

$$\mu = \frac{(k-l)(1-\lambda\gamma)+\overline{\sigma\beta}\left(1-\lambda^2\dfrac{S\overline{1-S}}{Q\overline{1-Q}}\right)}{1-\lambda\gamma+(\bar{\sigma}-1)\left(1-\lambda^2\dfrac{S\overline{1-S}}{Q\overline{1-Q}}\right)}. \qquad \ldots (2.31)$$

We can use the eleven equations (2.14) to (2.24) together with equations (2.28) and (2.30) to evaluate the rates of growth of the different variables in our economy in terms of l, r_c, r_m, and $\overline{\sigma\beta}$ and of the structural parameters of the system. We shall not give the solutions for all the variables concerned, but only for those in which we are especially interested, namely, for w, p, v, $y-l$, $c-l$, $m-l$, and q. $y-l$, $c-l$, and $m-l$ give the rate of growth in net income per head, consumption per head, and output of capital goods per head, and they can be taken as measures of change in the real standard of living, while q gives a measure of the rate of change in the distribution of the total real income between profits and wages.

The values of these rates of growth are given by the following equations[1], where $\mu = w-p-v$ has the value given in (2.31):

$$w = r_c+(1-Q_c)\mu \qquad \ldots (2.32)$$

$$p = r_c-r_m-\lambda\mu \qquad \ldots (2.33)$$

$$v = r_m-Q_m\mu \qquad \ldots (2.34)$$

$$\left.\begin{aligned} y-l &= (1-Q)(k-l)+r_c(1-S)+r_mS+Sp \\ &= (1-Q)(k-l)+r_c-S\lambda\mu \end{aligned}\right\} \qquad \ldots (2.35)$$

---

[1] We shall continue to write k, instead of $\dfrac{SY}{PK}$ from equation 2.28, for the rate of accumulation of machinery. This we do merely to simplify the expressions.

$$c - l = y - l + \frac{\gamma Q}{1 - S} q$$

$$= (k-l)(1-Q)\left(1 - \frac{\gamma Q}{1-S}\right) + r_c - \mu\left(\lambda S - \frac{\gamma Q \overline{1-Q}}{1-S}\right)$$

$$\ldots (2.36)$$

$$m - l = y - l - p - \frac{\gamma Q}{S} q$$

$$= (k-l)(1-Q)\left(1 + \frac{\gamma Q}{S}\right) + r_m + \mu\left(\lambda\overline{1-S} - \frac{\gamma Q \overline{1-Q}}{S}\right)$$

$$\ldots (2.37)$$

$$q = -(1-Q)(k-l-\mu). \qquad \ldots (2.38)$$

In the above equations we have not included the values of k_m, k_c, l_m, and l_c, because in the remainder of this Appendix we shall not be concerned with the way in which the supplies of machinery and of labour are distributed among the capital-goods industry and the consumption-goods industry. But in case any reader wishes to pursue this problem, the formulae for k_m, k_c, l_m, and l_c are as follows:

$$k_m = k\left(1-Q\right)\left(1 + \frac{\gamma Q}{S}\right) + lQ\left(1 - \frac{\gamma\overline{1-Q}}{S}\right)$$

$$+ \mu\left(\lambda\overline{1-S} - \frac{\gamma Q\overline{1-Q}}{S} + \sigma_m Q_m\right) - \sigma_m Q_m \beta_m.$$

$$k_c = k\left(1-Q\right)\left(1 - \frac{\gamma Q}{1-S}\right) + lQ\left(1 + \frac{\gamma\overline{1-Q}}{1-S}\right)$$

$$- \mu\left(\lambda S - \frac{\gamma Q\overline{1-Q}}{1-S} - \sigma_c Q_c\right) - \sigma_c Q_c \beta_c.$$

$$l_m = k\left(1-Q\right)\left(1 + \frac{\gamma Q}{S}\right) + lQ\left(1 - \frac{\gamma\overline{1-Q}}{S}\right)$$

$$+ \mu\left(\lambda\overline{1-S} - \frac{\gamma Q\overline{1-Q}}{S} - \sigma_m\overline{1-Q_m}\right) + \sigma_m \beta_m\overline{1-Q_m}.$$

$$l_c = k(1-Q)\left(1 - \frac{\gamma Q}{1-S}\right) + lQ\left(1 + \frac{\gamma\overline{1-Q}}{1-S}\right)$$

$$-\mu\left(\lambda S - \frac{\gamma Q\overline{1-Q}}{1-S} + \sigma_c\overline{1-Q_c}\right) + \sigma_c\beta_c\overline{1-Q_c}.$$

These equations can be used to derive the particular values of k_m, k_c, l_m, and l_c for the special cases examined later in this Appendix.

We can at this stage make some useful comments on the economic meaning of equations (2.31) to (2.38).

We have already explained that the value of μ (i.e. the extent to which the cost of using a unit of labour must rise relatively to that of using a machine) will depend essentially upon three factors (see pp. 135 and 136 above). Two of these are clearly illustrated in the equation for μ given in (2.31): First, a positive value of $k-l$ will mean that more machinery to labour must be used and, *ceteris paribus*, this will need a relative fall in the cost of employing machines to bring about the necessary substitution; second, a positive value of $\overline{\sigma\beta}$ will mean that technical progress is tending to raise the marginal importance in production of labour relatively to machinery. The third factor influencing the value of μ, which we discussed on page 136 above has now changed its form. Any shift of demand away from capital goods to consumption goods or *vice versa*, resulting from a change in the distribution of income and so a change in the proportions of income which are saved and spent is now built into our system and shows itself in (2.31) in the way in which the term γ (i.e. the excess of the proportion of profits saved over that of wages saved) modifies the effect of $k-l$ and of $\overline{\sigma\beta}$ upon μ. But in this connection there is one most important relationship which must be understood.

Consider the sign of the denominator of the right-hand side of equation (2.31), namely of

$$1 - \lambda\gamma + (\bar{\sigma} - 1)\left(1 - \lambda^2\frac{\overline{S1-S}}{\overline{Q1-Q}}\right).$$

We know that $1 - \lambda^2\dfrac{\overline{S1-S}}{\overline{Q1-Q}}$ is a positive fraction between 0 and 1 (see page 133 above). We know also that $1 - \lambda\gamma$ is positive, since both $|\lambda|$ and $|\gamma|$ are fractions lying between 0 and 1. If, therefore, $\bar{\sigma} > 1$, the denominator of equation (2.31) is certainly positive. But if $\bar{\sigma} < 1$, it is possible that the denominator of equation (2.31) is a negative quantity.

Consider an extreme possibility of this case. Suppose (i) that substitutability between the factors were negligible so that we could treat $\bar{\sigma}$ and $\overline{\sigma\beta}$ as equal to zero; and (ii) that all profits were saved ($S_v = 1$) and no wages were saved ($S_w = 0$) so that $\gamma = 1$ and $S = 1 - Q$. Then the denominator of the right-hand side of equation (2.31) would equal $-\lambda(1 - \lambda)$ and μ would have the following value:

$$\mu = \frac{k-l}{-\lambda}.$$

The denominator would be negative if $Q_c > Q_m$, i.e. if the consumption-good industries were more labour-intensive than the capital-good industries.

What is the economic implication of this? Let us suppose that machinery is being accumulated more quickly than labour is growing so that $k > l$. This would tend to make machines more abundant relatively to labour; and market forces would tend to cause the price for hiring labour to rise relatively to that of hiring machinery. But suppose that the possibilities of substituting machines for labour are small ($\bar{\sigma}$ is nearly zero). This change in relative factor prices will have little effect in inducing producers to use machines in the higher ratio to labour in which they are now available. The change in factor rewards will in this case shift income from profits to wages and this will cause a large fall in savings (since nearly all profits and practically no wages are saved). This will cause a shift of demand in the economy as a whole away from new capital goods for investment purposes on to consumption goods to match the reduced level of savings; and since consumption goods are assumed to be more labour-intensive than capital goods in their production, this will represent an indirect shift of demand away from the use of machinery (which is needed to produce capital goods) on to labour (which is needed to produce consumption goods). In other words, when the ratio of available machinery to available labour rises, the wage rate will tend to rise relatively to the cost of hiring a machine; this change in relative factor prices will have a double effect: first, it will tend to induce producers to use a higher ratio of machinery to labour and this will tend to restore equilibrium; second, it will cause a redistribution of income which, by affecting the proportion of income saved, will affect the relative demand for consumption goods and for capital goods, and this will tend to worsen the disequilibrium in the factor markets if it represents a shift of demand away from the less, on to the more, labour-intensive products. If the elasticity of substitution between the factors is much less than unity, if a large proportion of profits and a small proportion of wages is saved, and if consumption goods are much more labour-intensive than capital goods in production, then the second effect will be disequilibrating and will outweigh the first equilibrating force. The market forces which will make the wage-rate rise relatively to the cost of hiring a machine when labour becomes relatively scarce, will tend to increase the excess demand for labour; equilibrium would require that a relative scarcity of labour should be accompanied by a fall and not by a rise in wage-rates relatively to the cost of hiring a machine. In what follows we shall neglect this rather extreme possibility. We shall assume that the denominator of the right-hand side of equation (2.31) is positive, i.e. that

$$\lambda\gamma \; < \; \bar{\sigma}\left(1 - \lambda^2 \frac{S\mathrm{i} \overline{-S}}{Q\mathrm{i} \overline{-Q}}\right) + \lambda^2 \frac{S\mathrm{i} \overline{-S}}{Q\mathrm{i} - Q}.$$

Let us suppose then that there is a given rate of accumulation of machinery (k), a given rate of population growth (l) and a given degree of bias in technical progress ($\overline{\sigma\beta}$) and that the denominator on the right hand side of equation (2.31) is positive. Then market forces will require a given change in the ratio of cost of employing a unit of labour to that of employing a machine; μ will have a certain value depending upon the values of $k-l$, $\overline{\sigma\beta}$, and the structural parameters of the economy given in (2.31). Suppose μ to have the positive value of 10 per cent per annum. This rate of change in the relative costs of the two factors can be brought about by a 10 per cent rise in the wage-rate, a 10 per cent fall in the price of machinery, or a 10 per cent fall in the rate of profit, or by any combination of these three elements, since $\mu = w - p - v$.

Equation (2.31) tells us what determines the value of μ. Equations (2.32), (2.33), and (2.34) tell us what determines how much of this change in relative factor costs is brought about by a rise in the wage rate, a fall in the price of capital goods, or a fall in the rate of profit.

The factors which determine the distribution of μ between $w, -p$, and $-v$ fall into two groups: first, r_c and r_m, the degrees of technical progress in the two industries; and second, Q_c and Q_m, the labour-intensity of production in the two industries.

It is clear from equations (2.32) and (2.33) that a high rate of technical progress in the consumption goods industry tends to cause (i) a high rate of increase in the real wage rate (w) and (ii) a high rate of rise in the price of capital goods in terms of consumption goods (p). Both these are what one would expect. The wage rate is measured in terms of consumption goods; a rapid rise of productivity in the consumption goods industries would naturally, therefore, tend to cause a rapid rise in the real wage rate[1]. A high rate of technical progress in the consumption goods industries will in itself tend to lower the cost of consumption goods and so to raise the price of capital goods in terms of consumption goods (p).

Similarly, it is clear from equations (2.33) and (2.34) that a high rate of technical progress in the capital-goods industries tends to cause (i) a high rate of fall in the price of capital goods in terms of consumption goods (p) and (ii) a high rate of rise of the rate of profit itself (v). Technical progress in the capital-goods industries will clearly tend to lower the cost of producing such goods and thus their price in terms of consumption goods. A high rate of technical progress in the capital-goods industries is also in itself[2] a factor which tends to raise the rate of profit. In the capital-goods industries a stock of machines (i.e. of capital goods) is used as a factor of production to produce an output of capital goods; anything which raises the productivity of all factors of production in the capital-goods industries will, therefore, tend

---

[1] Any labour-saving bias in such inventions would show itself in a negative value for $\overline{\sigma\beta}$ and so in a lowered value of μ in equation (2.32).

[2] i.e. apart from any possible machinery-saving bias in such invention which would raise $\overline{\sigma\beta}$ and so tend to lower v through the consequential rise of μ in equation (2.34).

to raise the productivity of machines (i.e. of capital goods) in producing capital goods, i.e. to raise the rate of profit itself.

From (2.32), (2.33), and (2.34) we have:

$$\left. \begin{array}{c} w = r_c + (1 - Q_c)\mu \\ v + p = r_c - Q_c\mu \end{array} \right\} \quad \dots (2.39)$$

Suppose that machinery is accumulating more quickly than the population is growing in such a way that, given the structural parameters in equation (2.31), $\mu = 10$ per cent per annum. In other words, this year the cost of employing a unit of labour relatively to the cost of employing a machine must rise by 10 per cent in order to get the higher ratio of machinery to labour used in the economy. This can come about by a 7 per cent rise in the wage rate with a 3 per cent fall in the cost of employing a machine; or by means of a 4 per cent rise in the wage rate with a 6 per cent fall in the cost of employing a machine; or by any other similar combination. Which of these will happen?

Now W measures the real wage rate measured in terms of consumption goods and PV is the cost of employing a machine, measured in terms of consumption goods. w, therefore, measures the proportionate change in the cost of employing a unit of labour while $v + p$ measures the proportionate change in the cost of employing a machine. It is clear from (2.39) that apart from r_c the distribution of μ between w and $v + p$ depends solely on Q_c, the labour-intensity of the consumption goods industry. If r_c is great, then *pro tanto* both W and PV can rise much in absolute terms. But apart from this influence of rapid technical progress upon the absolute level of the rate of growth of wages and profits, it is clear from (2.39) that of μ a proportion $1 - Q_c$ will represent a rise in the cost of employing a unit of labour and the remaining proportion Q_c will represent a fall in the cost of employing a machine. In other words, if the consumption goods industries are very labour-intensive (Q_c large and $1 - Q_c$ small), then (technical progress apart) a given proportionate rise in the ratio of wages per worker to profits per machine must come about through a small rise in wages per worker and a large fall in profits per machine.

The reason for this is simple. Where wages make up most of the cost of producing a consumption good, a small proportionate rise in the wage rate in terms of consumption goods will cause quite a large rise in the cost of production of a consumption good.

In order that this should be balanced by an equivalent fall in the cost of production of a consumption good, there must be an equal fall in the profits per consumption good; but where profits make up only a small proportion of total costs, this involves a large proportionate fall in total profits and therefore in profits per machine. The point can be made very simply in the case of constant-returns production functions, such as we are assuming. In such a case we have

$$C = C(L_c, K_c)$$

and, since we have constant returns to scale,

$$C = C_l L_c + C_k K_c.$$

Differentiating these two equations we have

$$dC = C_l \, dL_c + C_k \, dK_c$$

and

$$dC = C_l \, dL_c + C_k \, dK_c + L_c \, dC_l + K_c \, dC_k.$$

Taking the difference between these two equations we have:

$$L_c \, dC_l = -K_c \, dC_k$$

or

$$\frac{C_k \, dC_l}{-C_l \, dC_k} = \frac{C_k K_c}{C_l L_c}$$

or

$$\frac{w}{-(p+v)} = \frac{1-Q_c}{Q_c}.$$

One can see the validity of this result from the following argument. Suppose that without any change in technical knowledge or in the supply of labour, one more machine is to be employed. This will involve some rise in the wage per worker and some fall in the profit per machine. But the new machine will be paid its marginal net product, i.e. the whole of the additional net product. Therefore the previous level of output must be divided between the previous number of machines and the previous number of workers. Therefore the total wage bill of the previous (and unchanged) number of workers must go up by the fall in the total amount of profits going to the previous number of machines. But if the previous wage bill were, say, twice as large as the previous total profit, then the wage bill of the previous workers and so the wage per worker will have to rise in a proportion which is only one half as great as the fall in the total of the previous profits earned by the previous number of machines, i.e. as the fall in the profit per machine.

While W and PV are the wage per worker and the profit per machine measured in terms of consumption goods, $\dfrac{W}{P}$ and V are the wage per worker and the profit per machine measured in terms of capital goods. In the capital goods industry, therefore, μ is distributed between a rise in wage per worker (measured in terms of capital goods, which are the product of industry) and a fall in profits per machine (measured in terms of capital goods). But if there are constant returns in the capital goods industries, then for reasons exactly similar to those given in the previous paragraphs, (if we abstract from the effect of technical progress—r_m—in raising the absolute level of both wages and profits in the capital-goods industry), the wage per worker (in terms of machines) will go up by $(1-Q_m)\mu$ while the profit per machine will go down by $Q_m\mu$. We can therefore generalise by saying that for the economy as a whole, abstracting from the effect of technical progress in raising both wages and profits, a 10 per cent rise in the ratio of wage per worker to profit per machine (i.e. a μ of 10 per cent per annum) will take the form mainly of a rise in wage per worker if total wages are a small proportion of total national income, but mainly in the form of a fall in profit per machine if wages make up a large proportion of total national income.

But while, apart from technical progress which can raise the absolute level of wages and profits, it is the absolute value of Q_c and Q_m which determines whether a change in factor prices takes the form mainly of a rise in wage per worker or of a fall in profit per machine, it is the difference between Q_c and Q_m which determines whether a fall in profit per machine (PV) takes the form mainly of a fall in the price of a machine (P) or of a fall in the rate of profit (V). We can see from (2.33) that $p = r_c - r_m - (Q_c - Q_m)\mu$. In other words, apart from any bias of technical progress between the two industries, the price of a machine will go down (or up) as a result of a rise in the wage per worker relatively to the profit per machine, according as consumption goods are more (or less) labour-intensive than capital goods to produce. In other words, if the wage per worker goes up relatively

145

to the profit per machine, then *ceteris paribus* the labour-intensive product will go up in cost and so in price relatively to the machinery-intensive product. But if the price of a machine actually rises, a given fall in the profit per machine would involve a very large fall in the rate of profit; whereas, if the price of a machine falls, a given fall in the profit per machine may involve only a small fall in the rate of profit.

To summarise, suppose an accumulation of machinery relatively to labour or a given labour-using bias in technical progress requires a 10 per cent rise in the wage per worker relatively to the profit per machine, this can occur: (i) with a large absolute rise in both wage per worker and profit per machine if the rate of technical progress is high (r_c and r_m large), (ii) with a large absolute rise in wage per worker and only a small absolute fall in profit per machine if total wages make up only a small part of total national income, and (iii) with any necessary fall in profit per machine taking the form of *either* a small fall in the rate of profit and a large fall in the price of a machine (if consumption goods are labour-intensive relatively to capital goods in production) *or* a large fall in the rate of profit and a small fall or even a rise in the price of a machine (if capital goods are more labour-intensive than consumption goods in production).

Let us next consider the economic meaning of equation (2.35). We know from page 16 of the main text that in a one-industry economy with two factors, constant returns to scale, and perfect competition

$$y - l = (1 - Q)(k - l)$$

or the rate of increase in output per head $(y - l)$ is equal to the rate of increase in machinery per head $(k - l)$ multiplied by the proportion of output which goes in profits to the owners of machines $(1 - Q)$.

If we now consider equation (2.35) in the form

$$y - l = (1 - Q)(k - l) + (1 - S)r_c + Sr_m + Sp,$$

we can see that for the economy as a whole, made up of two constant-returns industries (a capital-goods industry and a consumption-goods industry) the rate of increase in real national income per head will also be equal to the rate of increase in machinery per head $(k - l)$ multiplied by the proportion of the national income which goes to profits $(1 - Q)$, all this modified by the additional terms $(1 - S)r_c$, Sr_m and Sp. The terms $(1 - S)r_c$ and Sr_m allow for the fact that real output per head will also be rising because of technical progress in the consumption-goods industry (r_c) and in the capital-goods industry (r_m), these two rates of technical progress being weighted by the proportion of income spent on consumption goods $(1 - S)$ and on capital goods (S). Finally, the price of capital goods may be rising at a certain rate in terms of consumption goods; and real income per head, if it is measured in terms of consumption goods, may rise because that part of income which represents the output of capital goods may be rising in price in terms of consumption goods. This element in the rate of rise of income per head is equal to the rate of rise in the price of capital goods (p) weighted by the proportion of income which consists of the output of capital goods.

Equation (2.36) says that consumption per head $(c - l)$ will go up at the same rate as income per head $(y - l)$ except in so far as (i) there is a re-distribution of gross income going on between profits and wages $(q \neq 0)$ and (ii) the proportion of profits saved is not the same as the proportion of wages which is saved $(\gamma \neq 0)$. If income is shifting from profits to wages $(q > 0)$ and a larger proportion of wages than of profits is spent $(\gamma > 0)$, then consumption per head will be rising more quickly than income per head $(c - l > y - l)$.

From (2.37) it can be seen that the rate of growth of the output of capital goods per head will differ from that of income per head if either there is a change in the proportion of income which is saved $(\gamma q \neq 0)$, or there is a change in the price of capital goods in terms of consumption goods $(p \neq 0)$. A redistribution of income from, say, wages to profits will increase the proportion of income which is saved (if the proportion of profits saved is greater than the proportion of wages saved) and, if equilibrium is to be maintained, this would, at constant prices, involve a growth in the output of capital goods at a more rapid rate than that on the output of consumption goods. Suppose, however, that there were no change in the proportion of income saved, so that the value of investment grew at the same rate as the value of the national income. If the price of capital goods were rising $(p > 0)$, then the *volume* of the output of capital goods would be rising less quickly than the *value* of investment, so that the output of capital goods per head would be rising less quickly than the national income per head $(m-l < y-l)$.

From (2.38) it can be seen that the proportion of national income which is paid out in wages will be rising $(q > 0)$ if $\mu > k-l$. Using the value of μ from (2.31) and simplifying[1], we see that $q > 0$ if

$$(k-l)(\bar{\sigma}-1) < \overline{\sigma\beta}.$$

If there is no labour-saving or labour-using bias in technical progress, $(\overline{\sigma\beta} = 0)$, then an increase in machinery per head $(k-l > 0)$ will cause a redistribution of income in favour of wages $(q > 0)$ if the elasticity of substitution between the two factors is less than unity $(\bar{\sigma} < 1)$. This is a familiar result. If the ratio of machines to workers available for employment goes up by 10 per cent, the proportion of national income which goes to wages will rise only if a more than 10 per cent rise in wages per worker relatively to profits per machine is required to induce producers to change their techniques and to use a 10 per cent greater amount of machinery per worker. But in so far as there is any bias in technical progress which is itself tending to raise the marginal importance of labour relatively to that of machinery, the tendency for total wages to rise relatively to total profits will be *pro tanto* reinforced. Even if $\bar{\sigma}$ were somewhat greater than unity, a rise in machinery per worker available for employment might nevertheless be associated with a rise in the proportion of total gross income which was paid out in wages.

In this model we have taken l (the rate of growth of the population) as given and have derived, *inter alia*, the value of w (the rate of rise in the real wage rate which is compatible with the full employment of the available working population). But we could use this relationship in our model the other way round: we could take w as given at zero and ask what value of l would result. In this case we should be asking how quickly the demand for labour would grow (i.e. the size of l) at a given real wage rate (i.e. with $w = 0$).

With $w = 0$, $\mu = -(p+v)$; or from equations (2.33) and (2.34),

---

[1] On the assumption that the denominator on the right hand side of equation (2.31) is $+$ *ve* (See pages 139–141).

$$\mu = -\frac{r_c}{1-Q_c}.$$

Substituting this value of μ in (2.31) and re-arranging terms, we get:

$$l = k + \overline{\sigma\beta}\frac{1-\lambda^2\overline{\dfrac{S_1-S}{Q_1-Q}}}{1-\lambda\gamma} + \frac{r_c}{1-Q_c}\left\{1+(\bar{\sigma}-1)\frac{1-\lambda^2\overline{\dfrac{S_1-S}{Q_1-Q}}}{1-\lambda\gamma}\right\}.$$

In other words, at a constant real wage rate the demand for labour (l) would grow at the same rate as machinery accumulated for it to work with (k), except in so far as a labour-using bias in innovation ($\overline{\sigma\beta} > 0$) or a general rise of productivity in the production of consumption-goods ($r_c > 0$) tended to raise the real wage rate and thus to enable employment to rise more quickly than the stock of machinery without a net fall in the real wage rate.

We will now take the model described by equations (2.31) to (2.38) and consider some special cases of it.

(i) Let us first consider the case in which there is in effect only one industry, because the conditions of production in the consumption-goods industry are exactly the same as those in the capital-goods industry. This involves the following assumptions:

$$Q_c = Q_m \equiv Q$$
$$\sigma_c = \sigma_m \equiv \sigma$$
$$r_c = r_m \equiv r$$
$$\beta_c = \beta_m \equiv \beta.$$

If we make these assumptions we have the following results:

$$w - p - v(\equiv \mu) = \frac{k-l}{\sigma} + \beta$$

$$w = r + (1-Q)\left(\frac{k-l}{\sigma} + \beta\right)$$

$$p = 0$$

$$v = r - Q\left(\frac{k-l}{\sigma} + \beta\right)$$

$$y - l = r + (1-Q)(k-l)$$

$$c-l = r + \frac{1-Q}{1-S}\left\{\left(1-S_v+\frac{S_v-S}{\sigma}\right)(k-l)+(S_v-S)\beta\right\}$$

$$m-l = r + \frac{1-Q}{S}\left\{\left(S_v-\frac{S_v-S}{\sigma}\right)(k-l)-(S_v-S)\beta\right\}$$

$$q = (1-Q)\left\{\frac{1-\sigma}{\sigma}(k-l)+\beta\right\}.$$

It is to be observed that in this simple case (a) $p = 0$, because there is in effect only one product and (b) if the same proportion of profits as of wages were saved (so that $S_v = S_w = S$), $y-l = c-l = m-l = r+(1-Q)(k-l)$, so that income, consumption, and investment per head would all be growing at the same rate equal to the rate of technical progress plus the rate at which machinery per head was growing, this latter term being weighted by the importance of profits in the national income.

(ii) We will next take the special case for the conditions of thriftiness which Mrs Robinson has used, in which all profits and no wages are saved. In this case $S_v = 1$ and $S_w = 0$ so that $\gamma = 1$ and $S = 1-Q$. We then have:

$$w-p-v(\equiv \mu) = \frac{k-l+\bar{\sigma}\bar{\beta}(1+\lambda)}{\bar{\sigma}+\lambda(\bar{\sigma}-1)}$$

$$y-l = r_c + \frac{1-Q}{\bar{\sigma}+\lambda(\bar{\sigma}-1)}\{(k-l)(\bar{\sigma}+\lambda[\bar{\sigma}-2])-\bar{\sigma}\bar{\beta}\lambda(1+\lambda)\}$$

$$c-l = r_c + \frac{(1-Q)(1-\lambda)}{\bar{\sigma}+\lambda(\bar{\sigma}-1)}\{k-l+\bar{\sigma}\bar{\beta}(1+\lambda)\}$$

$$m-l = r_m + \frac{(k-l)\{\bar{\sigma}+\lambda(\bar{\sigma}-1)-Q(1-\lambda)\}-\bar{\sigma}\bar{\beta}Q(1+\lambda)(1-\lambda)}{\bar{\sigma}+\lambda(\bar{\sigma}-1)}$$

$$q = \frac{(1-Q)(1+\lambda)}{\bar{\sigma}+\lambda(\bar{\sigma}-1)}\{(k-l)(1-\bar{\sigma})+\bar{\sigma}\bar{\beta}\}$$

Further considerable simplifications can be obtained by taking special values for $\bar{\sigma}$ and λ.

(iii) We will next examine at rather greater length the case of fixed factor proportions, because this case has not been analysed so carefully by previous writers. We will suppose that there is no technical progress ($r_c = r_m = \beta_c = \beta_m = \overline{\sigma\beta} = 0$) but that machinery is accumulating at a different rate from the growth of population ($k - l \neq 0$). We ask now what happens if in each industry there is a fixed ratio between labour and machinery ($\sigma_c = \sigma_m = \bar{\sigma} = 0$). There can still be a moving equilibrium with full employment of labour and of machinery if the machinery-labour ratio is different in the two industries ($\lambda \neq 0$), because in this case the machinery-intensive industry can expand at the expense of the labour-intensive industry so that for the average of the economy as a whole the ratio of machinery to labour rises. In order to avoid the type of difficulty discussed on pages 139–141 above we shall add to our assumptions the supposition that a re-distribution of income does not affect the proportion of income which is saved ($S_v = S_w$ so that $\gamma = 0$).

In this case we have:

$$w - p - v \, (\equiv \mu) = (k-l)\frac{Q(1-Q)}{\lambda^2 S(1-S)}$$

$$w = (k-l)\frac{(1-Q_c)Q(1-Q)}{\lambda^2 S(1-S)}$$

$$p = -(k-l)\frac{Q(1-Q)}{\lambda S(1-S)}$$

$$v = -(k-l)\frac{Q_m Q(1-Q)}{\lambda^2 S(1-S)}$$

$$y - l = c - l = -(k-l)\frac{Q_m(1-Q)}{\lambda(1-S)}$$

$$m - l = (k-l)\frac{Q_c(1-Q)}{\lambda S}$$

$$q = (k-l)(1-Q)\frac{Q(1-Q) - \lambda^2 S(1-S)}{\lambda^2 S(1-S)}$$

$$= (k-l)(1-Q)\frac{(1-S)Q_c(1-Q_c) + SQ_m(1-Q_m)}{\lambda^2 S(1-S)}$$

Suppose that there is a certain rate of accumulation of machinery per head ($k > l$). There will be a tendency for wages per worker to rise relatively to the profits per machine. μ will be > 0 in the above equations. This will raise the cost of capital goods in terms of consumption goods if capital goods are the labour-intensive product and will lower the cost of capital goods if consumption goods are the labour-intensive product (p in the above equations has the opposite sign from λ). Suppose for the moment that capital goods are the labour-intensive product so that their cost goes up ($p > 0$). Then this will restore equilibrium if the rise in the price of capital goods in terms of consumption goods causes a shift of demand away from expensive capital goods on to cheap consumption goods, and thus causes an indirect shift of demand away from the labour needed to produce capital goods on to the machinery needed to produce consumption goods.

But since we are assuming that a fixed proportion of income is saved (regardless of its distribution between wages and profits), a rise in the price of capital goods in terms of consumption goods will cause a smaller number of capital goods to be purchased for investment purposes relatively to the number of consumption goods purchased for final consumption. In this case in which capital goods are the labour-intensive product ($\lambda < 0$), we can see from the above equations that $c - l$ is > 0 but $m - l$ is < 0. With a constant population the rise in the price of capital goods must be so great as to cause some absolute reduction in the number of capital goods purchased so as to release from the capital-goods industries some positive amount of labour (together with a very small amount of machinery) to be used with the newly accumulated machinery in the consumption-goods industries in order to make up a balanced equipment of machinery and labour to expand those industries. The new and higher overall balance of machinery to labour can be achieved only if there is some actual absolute contraction of the labour-intensive capital-goods industry to go with the expansion of the machinery-intensive consumption-goods industry.

In the converse case in which the consumption-goods industry was the labour-intensive industry ($\lambda > 0$), there would have to be an absolute contraction of the output of consumption goods to release labour to be employed with the newly accumulated machinery in the machine-intensive capital-goods industry. In this case the mechanism of adjustment would be on the following lines. The accumulation of machinery and the consequential relative scarcity of labour would tend to raise wages per worker and to lower profits per machine. This would lower the cost-price of machinery-intensive capital goods relatively to the cost-price of labour-intensive consumption goods. Out of a given and constant proportion of income saved a larger amount of the now cheap capital goods could be bought. The ratio of capital goods to consumption goods currently purchased would rise. This change in price would have to go on until more capital goods and less consumption goods were being bought in amounts which enabled the higher overall ratio of machinery to labour to be employed, by means of this contraction of the labour-intensive consumption-goods industry and the expansion of the machinery-intensive capital-goods industry.

It is to be observed that $y - l = c - l$. In other words, the real national income per head, measured in terms of consumption goods, would rise or fall at the same rate as the output of consumption goods per head of the population. This follows from our assumption that a constant proportion of income is spent on consumption goods; in this case if income measured in terms of consumption goods goes up (or down) by 1 per cent, then consumption also goes up (or down) by 1 per cent. It follows that in the case in which consumption goods are the labour-intensive product, so that the accumulation of machinery (as we have seen) involves an expansion of the machinery-intensive capital-goods industries and a contraction of the labour-intensive consumption-goods industries, not only will consumption per head fall, but national income per head measured in consumption goods will also fall. The national income measured in terms of consumption goods will fall, even though there is the same amount of labour and more machinery used in production in the economy as a whole. The output of consumption goods will fall; although the output of capital goods will rise to such an extent as to give employment to all factors of production, including the increased supply of machinery, yet the price of capital goods will fall so much in terms of consumption goods, that there is a net fall in the total income measured in terms of consumption goods.

This case in which capital accumulation leads to a steady fall in the standard of living is, of course, absurd. The absurdity lies in the fact that a constant proportion of the national income continues to be saved and devoted to the accumulation of machinery even though the net return on such investment is negative. The rate of return on investment is the rate of profit as we have defined it (V) plus the rate at which the market value of a machine is appreciating (p). Now $V = \dfrac{(1-Q)Y}{PK}$ or total profits divided by the value of the stock of machines; and if we write $k = \dfrac{SY}{PK}$ and $l = 0$, the value of p from the above equations is $-\dfrac{(1-Q)Y}{PK} \cdot \dfrac{Q}{\lambda(1-S)}$. Making use of (2.13) we see that

$$V + p = -\frac{(1-Q)Y}{PK} \cdot \frac{Qm}{\lambda(1-S)},\text{so that when } \lambda > 0, V+p \text{ is} < 0.$$

The common sense of this conclusion is apparent. We are now dealing with the case in which $\dfrac{K_m}{L_m} > \dfrac{K}{L} > \dfrac{K_c}{L_c}$; that is to say, (i) the capital-good industry is assumed to be more machine-intensive than the consumption-good industry $\left(\dfrac{K_m}{L_m} > \dfrac{K_c}{L_c}\right)$, but (ii) since there can be full employment of K and of L only if $\dfrac{K}{L}$ is a weighted average of $\dfrac{K_m}{L_m}$ and $\dfrac{K_c}{L_c}$, we must confine our attention to the cases where $\dfrac{K}{L}$ happens to lie between $\dfrac{K_m}{L_m}$ and $\dfrac{K_c}{L_c}$. But as soon as capital accumulation has proceeded to the point at which $\dfrac{K}{L}$ is as great as $\dfrac{K_c}{L_c}$, then (with a constant L) all further capital accumulation is a mere waste of resources. For as soon as $\dfrac{K}{L} = \dfrac{K_c}{L_c}$, all the available labour (L) can be employed to produce consumption goods with a full complement of co-operating machinery (K). With a rigidly fixed ratio of K_c to L_c, there is no point in devoting further resources to the production of more machinery since in the absence of a greater total labour supply no more consumption goods can be produced.

Finally, it is to be observed that if $|\lambda|$ is small all the changes in the economy will have to be on a very large scale to preserve equilibrium. If the ratio of labour to machinery does not differ much between the two industries, there will have to be a very large expansion in the machinery-intensive industry and a very large contraction in the labour-intensive industry in order to obtain a given increase in the overall average ratio of machinery to labour in use throughout the economy. To bring this about there will have to be a very large change in the price of capital goods in terms of consumption goods and a very large rise in the real wage rate and fall in the rate of profit. At the extreme, as $|\lambda|$ approaches zero, the smallest increase in machinery per head would reduce the rate of profit to zero and raise the rate of wages to absorb the whole national income. Machinery would become a free good and the additional supply of it would remain unemployed.

(iv) We will now consider a peculiarly important special case. If in any industry (a) the elasticity of substitution is unity and (b) technical progress is, as we have defined it, neither labour-saving nor labour-using, then the distribution of the product of that industry between wages and profits will remain constant. We have already examined the reasons for this above (see pages 30–32). Let us suppose this to be the case in both of our industries, so that $\sigma_c = \sigma_m = \bar{\sigma} = 1$ and $\beta_c = \beta_m = \bar{\sigma}\bar{\beta} = 0$. Then we have:

$$w - p - v \; (\equiv \mu) = k - l$$
$$w = y - l = c - l = r_c + (1 - Q_c)(k - l)$$
$$p = r_c - r_m - \lambda(k - l)$$
$$v = r_m - Q_m(k - l)$$
$$m - l = r_m + (1 - Q_m)(k - l)$$
$$q = 0.$$

This is, *par excellence*, the constant-proportion case. The ratio of total wages to total profits remains unchanged ($q = 0$). Since there is no change in the distribution of total national income, the ratio of total savings to total income remains unchanged; and as a result the ratio of consumption to real national income remains unchanged (i.e. $y - l = c - l$). But as the ratio of total wages to total national income remains unchanged (since $q = 0$), it follows that wages per head move in the same proportion as total income per head ($w = y - l$).

In an economy in which all these basic proportions remain constant we can in fact go much further in our analysis than we have done so far. Up to this point we have been examining only the relationships which must exist at any one moment of time between the rates of growth of the different variables in order to keep the system in moving equilibrium. We have said nothing more about the pattern of the movement of any one of these variables through time. For this purpose we should have to integrate the rate of change of the variable and thus observe the absolute value of the variable at different moments of time. In an economy in which the distribution of income in each industry as well as in the economy as a whole is constant, we can take this further step. This constant-proportion special case is thus of exceptional importance, and we shall devote a whole new model to it.

(3) THREE FACTORS WITH A CONSTANT DISTRIBUTION OF INCOME

This model is so important that we shall start again *ab initio*. We no longer assume that there are constant returns to scale or that there are only two factors of production. The basic assumption which we make is that in each industry the substitutability between the factors of production, the nature of technical progress, and the market conditions are together such that in our private-enterprise economy equilibrium will be maintained only when the distribution of net income in each industry is constant. A special case of this is, as we have seen, where the elasticity of substitution between any two factors is unity, where technical progress is neither labour-using nor labour-saving, and where there is perfect competition so that factors are paid rewards equal to the value of their marginal products. For the moment, however, we simply assume that in each industry the proportion of the net income which goes to any one factor is kept constant by the forces of the market. What are the implications of this?

Consider the following twelve equations, where the unexplained terms have the same meaning as in the previous model.

$$K = K_m + K_c \qquad \ldots (3.1)$$

$$L = L_m + L_c \qquad \ldots (3.2)$$

$$N = N_m + N_c \qquad \qquad \cdots (3.3)$$

where N is the total amount of land (or natural resources) available for employment and N_m and N_c shows its distribution between the capital-goods and the consumption-goods industries.

$$WL_m = Q_m MP \qquad \qquad \cdots (3.4)$$

$$WL_c = Q_c C \qquad \qquad \cdots (3.5)$$

$$PVK_m = U_m MP \qquad \qquad \cdots (3.6)$$

$$PVK_c = U_c C \qquad \qquad \cdots (3.7)$$

$$GN_m = (1 - Q_m - U_m)MP \qquad \cdots (3.8)$$

$$GN_c = (1 - Q_c - U_c)C \qquad \cdots (3.9)$$

where Q_m, U_m, and $1 - Q_m - U_m$ are the proportions of the income earned in the capital-goods industry which goes to wages, profits, and rents respectively and similarly for Q_c, U_c, and $1 - Q_c - U_c$ in the consumption-goods industry; and where G is the rent per acre of land measured in terms of consumption goods. We assume that Q_m, Q_c, U_m, and U_c are all constant.

To these we can add three 'social-accounting' equations:

$$MP = SY \qquad \qquad \cdots (3.10)$$

$$Y = MP + C \qquad \qquad \cdots (3.11)$$

$$SY = S_w WL + S_v(Y - WL). \qquad \cdots (3.12)$$

These three equations state: that the value of investment equals the national income multiplied by the proportion of income which is saved; that income is made up of consumption plus investment; and that savings are equal to the wage-bill multiplied by the proportion of wages which is saved plus the non-wage remainder of income multiplied by the proportion of non-wage income which is saved.

Equations (3.2), (3.4), and (3.5) give us $WL = Q_m MP + Q_c C$; by means of this equation and equations (3.10), (3.11), and (3.12) we obtain:

$$S = \frac{S_v(1 - Q_c) + S_w Q_c}{1 - (S_v - S_w)(Q_c - Q_m)}. \qquad \cdots (3.13)$$

We are assuming in this model that Q_c and Q_m are constant. If, as in the previous model, we also assume that S_v and S_w are constant, it follows that S is constant also. Since $Q = SQ_m + (1-S)Q_c$ (see (2.13) on page 127 above), it follows also that Q is constant. The constancy of S, Q_m, Q_c, U_m, and U_c will play a central role in the development of this model.

We can proceed by rearranging the eight equations (3.4) to (3.11) to obtain:

$$
\left.
\begin{aligned}
WL_m &= Q_m S Y \\
WL_c &= Q_c(1-S)Y \\
PVK_m &= U_m S Y \\
PVK_c &= U_c(1-S)Y \\
GN_m &= (1-Q_m-U_m)SY \\
GN_c &= (1-Q_c-U_c)(1-S)Y \\
MP &= SY \\
C &= (1-S)Y
\end{aligned}
\right\} \quad \dots (3.14)
$$

Remembering that S, Q_m, Q_c, U_m, and U_c are all constant we can differentiate (3.14) to obtain:

$$
\left.
\begin{aligned}
y &= w+l_m \\
y &= w+l_c \\
y &= p+v+k_m \\
y &= p+v+k_c \\
y &= g+n_m \\
y &= g+n_c \\
y &= m+p \\
y &= c
\end{aligned}
\right\} \quad \dots (3.15)
$$

where the small letters have the same meaning as in the previous model, i.e. $y = \dfrac{1}{Y}\dfrac{dY}{dt}$ etc.

From the first two of these equations we can see that $l_m = l_c$ and, similarly, from the following four equations that $k_m = k_c$ and $n_m = n_c$. The economic meaning of this is clear. Since a constant proportion of income is saved, the ratio of the value of investment to the value of consumption will be constant. But since the wage-bill in the capital-goods industry is a constant proportion (Q_m) of the value of the output of that industry, and since the wage-bill in the consumption-goods industry is a constant proportion (Q_c) of the value of the output of that industry, the wage-bill in the capital-goods industry (WL_m) will bear a constant ratio to the wage-bill in the consumption-goods industry (WL_c). But since the wage per worker will be the same in both industries, the ratio of employment in the one industry to employment in the other will remain constant. In other words, the proportionate rate of growth of employment in the one industry will equal the proportionate rate of growth of employment in the other (i.e. $l_m = l_c$). But since these are the only industries and full employment is assumed throughout, this rate of growth must be equal to the rate of growth of the total population, or $l_m = l_c = l$. By a similar reasoning we have $k_m = k_c = k$ and $n_m = n_c = n$. But since the total amount of land N is constant, we have in this latter case, $n_m = n_c = 0$. To summarise:

$$\left. \begin{array}{l} l_m = l_c = l \\ k_m = k_c = k \\ n_m = n_c = 0 \end{array} \right\} \quad \ldots (3.16)$$

The eleven equations in (3.15) and (3.16) express the basic and simple relationships between the various rates of growth in an economy in which the distributions of income Q_c, Q_m, U_c, and U_m and the savings propensities S_w and S_p are all constant. They constitute the fundamental simplicity of this 'constant-proportions' economy which we shall now proceed to analyse in more detail.

We have not needed until now in this 'constant-proportions' model to introduce any production functions. This we must now do for each of our two industries:

$$\left. \begin{array}{l} M = M(K_m, L_m, N_m, t) \\ C = C(K_c, L_c, N_c, t) \end{array} \right\} \quad \ldots (3.17)$$

We do not at this stage necessarily assume there to be constant returns to scale. In this respect our model is more general than the previous one. Differentiating the equation for M and remembering from (3.16) that $k_m = k$, $l_m = l$, and $n_m = 0$, we have

$$m = \bar{Q}_m l + \bar{U}_m k + r_m \qquad \ldots (3.18)$$

159

where $\bar{Q}_m = \dfrac{L_m(\partial M/\partial L_m)}{M}$ or the proportion of the value of the output of capital goods which would go to wages in that industry *if* labour were paid a reward equal to the value of its marginal product. We may call this the proportionate marginal product of labour in the capital-goods industry. Similarly, $\bar{U}_m$ is the proportionate marginal product of machinery in the capital-goods industry or the proportion of the value of the output of capital goods which would go to gross profits in that industry if machinery did receive a reward in that industry equal to the value of its marginal product. In what follows we shall assume that $\bar{Q}_m$ and $\bar{U}_m$ are constant, just as we have assumed that Q_m and U_m are constant. But we do not necessarily assume that $\bar{Q}_m = Q_m$ or $\bar{U}_m = U_m$[1]. In other words factors receive a reward which is a constant proportion of the total output and which also bears a constant ratio to the value of their marginal product; but their reward is not necessarily equal to the value of their marginal product.

Similarly for C from (3.17):

$$c = \bar{Q}_c l + \bar{U}_c k + r_c. \qquad \ldots (3.19)$$

We can now, from the equations in (3.15), (3.16), (3.18), and (3.19) obtain expressions for the various rates of growth in our economy in terms of r_c, r_m, k, l and the proportional marginal products $\bar{Q}_c$, $\bar{Q}_m$, $\bar{U}_c$, and $\bar{U}_m$. These are as follows:

$$\left.\begin{aligned} y = c = g &= r_c + \bar{Q}_c l + \bar{U}_c k \\ m &= r_m + \bar{Q}_m l + \bar{U}_m k \\ p\,(= c - m) &= r_c - r_m + (\bar{Q}_c - \bar{Q}_m)l + (\bar{U}_c - \bar{U}_m)k \\ w\,(= y - l) &= r_c - (1 - \bar{Q}_c)l + \bar{U}_c k \\ v\,(= m - k) &= r_m + \bar{Q}_m l - (1 - \bar{U}_m)k \end{aligned}\right\} \qquad \ldots (3.20)$$

It may be observed from (3.20) that $w - p - v\,(= \mu) = k - l$ (which was the value obtained for μ at the end of Section (2) on page 155 above).

We shall take the rates of technical progress (r_m and r_c) and the rate of population growth (l) as given and constant. We have,

---

[1] In our previous model $Q_m = \bar{Q}_m = 1 - \bar{U}_m = 1 - U_m$ and $Q_c = \bar{Q}_c = 1 - \bar{U}_c = 1 - U_c$.

therefore, in (3.20) expressed the various rates of growth in our economy (y, c, m, p, w, v, and g) in terms of the constants $\bar{Q}_c$, $\bar{Q}_m$, $\bar{U}_c$, $\bar{U}_m$, r_c, r_m, and l and of the rate of growth of the stock of machinery, k. In the previous model we could say only that at any one moment of time k would be equal to $\dfrac{SY}{KP}$ (see (2.28) above).

But in this 'constant-proportions' world we can in fact exactly describe the time-path of k itself (and so of the rates of growth of our other variables) in terms of our given constants. Moreover, from the time-path of the rate of growth of the stock of machinery (k) we can derive the time-path of the stock of machinery itself (K) and so the time-path of our original variables themselves (namely, of M, C, Y, P, W, V, and G). We shall then have a complete theory of the movement of an economic system in equilibrium through time.

Let us, then, consider the movement of k through time. Since M (i.e. the output of capital goods available for net investment) equals $\dfrac{dK}{dt}$ (i.e. the rate of increase in the stock of machinery), we have

$$k = \frac{M}{K}. \qquad \ldots (3.21)$$

Differentiating this, we have

$$\frac{dk}{dt} = k(m-k)$$

$$= k\{r_m + \bar{Q}_m l - (1 - \bar{U}_m)k\} \text{ (from (3.20))}$$

$$= -(1 - \bar{U}_m)k^2 + \{(r_m + \bar{Q}_m l)\}k. \qquad \ldots (3.22)$$

If we then integrate $\dfrac{dk}{dt}$ in (3.22), we have:

$$k = \frac{k_0 \exp[(r_m + \bar{Q}_m l)t]}{1 + k_0 \dfrac{1 - \bar{U}_m}{r_m + \bar{Q}_m l}\{\exp[(r_m + \bar{Q}_m l)t] - 1\}} \qquad \ldots (3.23)$$

Equation (3.23) has a number of important properties. We will mention four of these and then comment on their economic significance:

First, in (3.23) as $t \to \infty$, so $k \to \dfrac{r_m + \bar{Q}_m l}{1 - \bar{U}_m}$.

Second, in (3.23) if $k_0 = \dfrac{r_m + \bar{Q}_m l}{1 - \bar{U}_m}$, then $k = k_0 = $ constant.

Third, if $r_m = l = 0$ (i.e. if there is no technical progress and no growth of population, so that we are considering the pure case of growth by capital accumulation), then

$$k = k_0 \frac{1}{1 + k_0(1 - \bar{U}_m)t}$$

so that k would continuously fall.

Fourth, in equation (3.23) it will be seen that only the conditions of production in the capital-goods industries (r_m, $\bar{Q}_m$, and $\bar{U}_m$) are relevant to the value of k. The conditions of production in the consumption-goods industries (r_c, $\bar{Q}_c$, and $\bar{U}_c$) do not appear in the equation.

Let us comment on the economic meaning of these features of equation (3.23). We may start by asking in what conditions k, the rate of growth of the stock of machinery, will be constant. Now M (i.e. the output of capital goods) represents the net addition to the stock of machines, so that $\dfrac{M}{K}$ represents k, the rate of growth of the stock of machinery K; and $\dfrac{M}{K}$ will be constant if the output of capital goods grows at the same rate as the stock of machines (i.e. if $m = k$).

In what conditions will this be so? Suppose that the stock of machinery increases by a proportion k; in what circumstances will the output of capital goods increase by this same proportion k? Because of the 'constant-proportions' assumptions of our model, equilibrium will be maintained when the total stock of machinery goes up by k, only if the stock of machinery used in the capital goods industries goes up by the same proportion k (i.e. $k_m = k$). (See equations (3.16) and the discussion of them on pages 158 and 159). But if the stock of machinery used to produce capital goods goes up by a proportion k, this itself will cause M, the output of capital goods, to go up by a proportion $\bar{U}_m$ times k, since $\bar{U}_m$ is the proportionate marginal product of K in producing M (see equation (3.18)). But if the output of capital goods, M, is to grow not by $\bar{U}_m k$ but by k other causes of growth must cause the output of capital goods to rise by a proportion $k(1 - \bar{U}_m)$. These other possible factors are (a) r_m, the rate of growth of the output of capital goods due to technical progress, and (b) $\bar{Q}_m l_m$, the rate of growth of the output of capital goods due to the rate of growth of employment (l_m) in the capital-goods industry multiplied by the proportional marginal product of labour in that industry ($\bar{Q}_m$). But our 'constant-proportions' assumptions means that the rate of growth of labour must be the same in both industries, so that $l_m = l$. We may conclude, therefore, that if $r_m + \bar{Q}_m l$ (the rate of growth of the output of capital goods due to other factors) plus $k\bar{U}_m$ (the rate of growth of the output of capital goods due to the accumulation of machinery) is equal to k (the rate of growth of the stock of machines), then the rate of growth of the output of capital goods will equal the rate of growth of the stock of machines, so that the rate of growth of the stock of machines will itself be constant. In other words, k is constant if $k = \dfrac{r_m + \bar{Q}_m l}{1 - U_m}$.

None of this argument depends upon the conditions of production in the consumption-goods industries. The argument depends vitally, as we have seen, upon our 'constant-proportions' assumptions which imply that if equilibrium is to be maintained the rate of growth of employment in the consumption-goods industries must be the same as the rate of growth of employment in the capital-goods industries and the rate of growth of the stock of machines in use in the consumption-goods industries must be the same as in the capital-goods industries. But given the maintenance of this distribution of the factors between the two industries, the rate of accumulation of machinery depends only upon how much the output of machinery will rise, i.e. upon the conditions of production in the machine-making industry. The conditions of production in the consumption-goods industry (r_c, $\bar{Q}_c$, and $\bar{U}_c$) will, of course, affect the rate of growth of the output of consumption goods which will be associated with any given rate of growth in the stock of machinery and in population and will, therefore, as we shall see, be very relevant in determining the rate of growth of real income, wages, the price of capital goods in terms of consumption goods, and so on. But given its initial value (k_0), the time path of the rate of growth of the stock of machinery (k) is determined solely by the conditions of production in the capital-goods industries.

But we must look a little more closely into the factors determining k_0, i.e. into the factors determining the rate of growth of the stock of machinery at any one given point of time. Now as we have seen $k = \dfrac{M}{K}$. But in order that the economy should be in equilibrium at any one point of time the output of capital goods (M) multiplied by their cost-price (P) must be equal to the national income (Y) multiplied by the proportion of that income which people wish to save (S) or $MP = SY$ (see equation (3.10)). In other words, in equilibrium, $M = \dfrac{SY}{P}$ or $k = S\dfrac{Y}{KP}$, where S is a given constant. (See equation (2.28).) Therefore,

$$k \gtreqqless \frac{r_m + \bar{Q}_m l}{1 - \bar{U}_m}$$

according as

$$\frac{Y}{KP} \gtreqqless \frac{r_m + \bar{Q}_m l}{S(1 - \bar{U}_m)} \qquad \ldots (3.24)$$

where the right-hand side of the inequality is a constant. If therefore, we start with an original ratio of income to the value of capital $\left(\dfrac{Y_0}{K_0 P_0}\right)$ which is greater than the right-hand side of (3.24) the rate of accumulation of machinery (k) will be greater than its ultimate value $\dfrac{r_m + \bar{Q}_m l}{1 - U_m}$ and it will be falling towards this ultimate value. The rate of accumulation of machinery will in fact be so high relatively to the rate of technical progress and the rate of population growth that 'diminishing returns' to the accumulation of machinery will be evident; the ratio of income to the value of the capital stock $\left(\dfrac{Y}{KP}\right)$ will be falling. This will go on until $\dfrac{Y}{KP}$ has fallen to the level given by the right-hand side of (3.24) and until k has fallen to $\dfrac{r_m + \bar{Q}_m l}{1 - \bar{U}_m}$. From

that point onwards k and $\dfrac{Y}{KP}$ will be constant.

If, however, there were no technical progress ($r_m = 0$) and no population growth ($l = 0$), then this point would never be reached. So long as there was any net capital accumulation k would remain $> \dfrac{r_m + \bar{Q}_m l}{1 - \bar{U}_m}$ and $\dfrac{Y}{KP}$ would remain $> \dfrac{r_m + \bar{Q}_m l}{S(1 - \bar{U}_m)}$, both of which

expressions would in this case be zero. Thus both k and $\dfrac{Y}{KP}$

would continue to fall towards zero as the process of diminishing returns to machinery due to the simple accumulation of capital operated in the economy.

But if r_m and l are not zero, there is, as we have seen, a constant

value of k, namely $\dfrac{r_m + \bar{Q}_m l}{1 - \bar{U}_m}$, to which k will tend as time elapses.

This represents the value of k in the state of steady growth to which the economy will tend. By substituting this value of k in equations (3.20), we obtain the following values for the growth rates of the variables in our economy when it has attained this state of steady growth:

$$
\left.
\begin{aligned}
y = c &= r_c + \bar{Q}_c l + \frac{\bar{U}_c}{1 - \bar{U}_m}(r_m + \bar{Q}_m l) \\[1em]
m = k &= \frac{r_m + \bar{Q}_m l}{1 - \bar{U}_m} \\[1em]
p = c - m &= r_c + \bar{Q}_c l - \frac{1 - \bar{U}_c}{1 - \bar{U}_m}(r_m + \bar{Q}_m l) \\[1em]
w = y - l &= r_c - (1 - \bar{Q}_c)l + \frac{\bar{U}_c}{1 - \bar{U}_m}(r_m + \bar{Q}_m l) \\[1em]
v = m - k &= 0 \quad \text{(i.e. } V \text{ is a constant)} \\[1em]
y - k - p &= 0 \quad \text{(i.e. } \tfrac{Y}{KP} \text{ is a constant)}
\end{aligned}
\right\} \quad \dots (3.25)
$$

We can now take another major step in our analysis. Equation (3.23) gives us the time path of k, the rate of growth of the stock of machinery. By integration, if we know the original stock of machinery (K_0), we can determine what the actual stock of machinery will be at any one moment of time. If we write $k_0 = \dfrac{SY_0}{K_0P_0}$ in equation (3.23) and integrate, we obtain:

$$\frac{K}{K_0} = \left\{ 1 + \frac{Y_0}{K_0P_0} \cdot \frac{S(1 - \bar{U}_m)}{r_m + \bar{Q}_m l}(\exp[(r_m + \bar{Q}_m l)t] - 1) \right\}^{1/1 - \bar{U}m} \dots (3.26)$$

It is to be observed that if $k_0 = \dfrac{r_m + \bar{Q}_m l}{1 - \bar{U}_m}$ and, therefore,

$$\frac{Y_0}{K_0P_0} = \frac{r_m + \bar{Q}_m l}{S(1 - \bar{U}_m)},$$

then $\dfrac{K}{K_0} = \exp(k_0 t)$. In other words, as we have already seen, if $k_0 = \dfrac{r_m + \bar{Q}_m}{1 - \bar{U}_m}$, then K grows at the constant rate k_0.

Equation (3.26) gives us the size of K at any point of time in terms of the initial size of K_0, Y_0, and P_0 and of the constants S, r_m, $\bar{Q}_m$, $\bar{U}_m$, and l. We are now in a position to derive the time paths of the other variables in our system.

Let us start with M. If $\bar{Q}_m$, $\bar{U}_m$, and r_m in equation (3.18) are constant, then the production function for M in (3.17) must be of the form

$$M = R_m \exp(r_m t) L_m{}^{\bar{Q}m} K_m{}^{\bar{U}m} \qquad \dots (3.27)$$

where R_m is a constant which measures the amount of M which would be produced at time o by one unit of L and one unit of K together with the constant amount of N—namely

$$\frac{S(1 - Q_m - U_m)N}{1 - Q - U}$$

—which will always be used in the production of M. Now since in our 'constant-proportions' system the proportion of the total population which is in the capital-goods industry is constant and the proportion of the stock of machinery which is used in this industry is constant (see (3.16)) we have $K_m = \dfrac{K_{m0}}{K_0}K$ and L_m

$= L_{m0} \exp(lt)$. Substituting these values of K_m and L_m in (3.27) we have

$$M = R_m L_{m0}{}^{\bar{Q}m} K_{m0}{}^{\bar{U}m} \exp[(r_m + \bar{Q}_m l)t]\left(\frac{K}{K_0}\right)^{\bar{U}m}$$

$$= M_0 \exp[(r_m + Q_m l)t]\left(\frac{K}{K_0}\right)^{\bar{U}m}$$

or, since $M_0 P_0 = Y_0 S$,

$$M = \frac{Y_0}{P_0} S. \; \exp[(r_m + \bar{Q}_m l)t]\left(\frac{K}{K_0}\right)^{\bar{U}m} \qquad \ldots (3.28)$$

where $\dfrac{K}{K_0}$ has the value given in (3.26).

From a precisely similar production function for C:

$$C = R_c \exp(r_c t) L_c{}^{\bar{Q}c} K_c{}^{\bar{U}c} \qquad \ldots (3.29)$$

we obtain:

$$C = Y_0 (1 - S) \exp[(r_c + \bar{Q}_c l)t]\left(\frac{K}{K_0}\right)^{\bar{U}c} \qquad \ldots (3.30)$$

Now we know that $Y = \dfrac{C}{1 - S}$, so that[1]

---

[1] Mr Kaldor's 'Technical Progress Function' (on page 604 of the *Economic Journal* for December 1937) is of the form $y = \alpha'' + \beta'' k$, where α'' and β'' are constants and the equation states that technical progress is such as to make the growth rate of output (y) a linear function of the growth rate of capital (k). This can be integrated into the simple production function

$$Y = Y_0 \exp(\alpha'' t)\left(\frac{K}{K_0}\right)^{\beta''}.$$

One of Mr Kaldor's main contentions is that we should not make use of a production function which is simply shifted through time by technical progress (i.e. that we should not express output as a function of two separate variables K—the factor of production—and t—time), because technical progress and the rate of capital accumulation are too intimately interwoven to make this separation useful. But in order to maintain this position he should logically choose a function relating the growth rate of output to the growth rate of capital of a kind which cannot be integrated. The particular criticism made in this footnote of Mr Kaldor's article is largely a debating point. He can well reply that his analysis is valid whether or not the technical progress function can be integrated, whereas the production function method can be used only in the former case.

$$Y = Y_0 \exp[(r_c + \check{Q}_c l)t]\left(\frac{K}{K_0}\right)^{\bar{U}_c}. \qquad \ldots (3.31)$$

We also know that $Y = \dfrac{C}{1-S} = \dfrac{MP}{S}$ or that $P = \dfrac{S}{1-S}\dfrac{C}{M}$, so that from (3.28) and (3.30):

$$P = P_0 \exp\{(r_c - r_m - [\check{Q}_c - \check{Q}_m]l)t\}\left(\frac{K}{K_0}\right)^{\bar{U}_c - \bar{U}m}. \qquad \ldots (3.32)$$

From the first two equations in (3.14) we know that

$$WL = \{Q_m S + Q_c(1-S)\}Y = QY,$$

where Q is the constant proportion of the national income which goes to wages. We also know that $L = L_0 \exp(lt)$ so that $W = \exp(-lt)\dfrac{YQ}{L_0}$ or, from (3.31)

$$W = \frac{Y_0}{L_0}Q. \ \exp\{(r_c - [1 - \check{Q}_c]l)t\}\left(\frac{K}{K_0}\right)^{\bar{U}_c} \qquad \ldots (3.33)$$

Similarly, from the second and third equations in (3.14) we know that $PVK = UY$, where U is the constant proportion of the national income which goes to profits. Therefore,

$$V = \frac{U}{PK}Y = \frac{U}{K_0}\frac{K_0}{U}\frac{Y}{P}$$

or from (3.31) and (3.32)

$$V = \frac{Y_0}{K_0 P_0}U \ \exp[(r_m + \check{Q}_m l)t]\left(\frac{K}{K_0}\right)^{-(1 - \bar{U}m)} \qquad \ldots (3.34)$$

And similarly from the fourth and fifth equations in (3.14) we know that $GN = (1 - Q - U)Y$ where $1 - Q - U$ is the constant proportion of the national income which goes to rent of land. Since $N = N_0 = $ constant, we have $G = \dfrac{1 - Q - U}{N_0}Y$ or from equation (3.31)

$$G = \frac{Y_0}{N_0}(1 - Q - U) \ \exp[(r_c + \check{Q}_c l)t]\left(\frac{K}{K_0}\right)^{\bar{U}_c} \qquad \ldots (3.35)$$

Thus equations (3.26), (3.28), and (3.30) to (3.34) enable us to determine the values at any time of K, M, C, Y, P, W, V, and G in terms of the constants S, Q, U, l, r_c, r_m, $\bar{Q}_c$, $\bar{Q}_m$, $\bar{U}_c$, and $\bar{U}_m$ and of the five initial values K_0, L_0, N_0, Y_0, and P_0.

In fact, given the three original factor supplies (K_0, L_0, and N_0) the original values of Y_0 and P_0 will already be determined. We know (from (3.2) and the first two equations in (3.14)) that

$$L_m = \frac{SQ_m}{SQ_m + (\mathrm{I} - S)Q_c}L \text{ or } L_m = \frac{SQ_m}{Q}L,$$

where S, Q_m, and Q are all constants. Similarly

$$L_c = \frac{(\mathrm{I} - S)Q_c}{Q}L, \quad K_m = \frac{SU_m}{U}K, \quad K_c = \frac{(\mathrm{I} - S)U_c}{U}K.$$

Substituting these values of L_m, L_c, K_m and K_c in the two production functions (3.27) and (3.29) we have

$$M_0 = R_m\left(\frac{SQ_mL_0}{Q}\right)^{\bar{Q}_m}\left(\frac{SU_mK_0}{U}\right)^{\bar{U}_m}$$

and

$$C_0 = R_c\left(\frac{[\mathrm{I} - S]Q_cL_0}{Q}\right)^{\bar{Q}_c}\left(\frac{[\mathrm{I} - S]U_cK_0}{U}\right)^{\bar{U}_c}.$$

We know that $P_0 = \dfrac{S}{\mathrm{I} - S}\dfrac{C_0}{M_0}$. (See the derivation of P in equation (3.32)) and that $Y_0 = \dfrac{C_0}{\mathrm{I} - S}$. (See the derivation of Y in equation (3.31).) We can thus express Y_0 and P_0 in terms of L_0 and K_0 and of the constants R_m, R_c, Q_m, Q_c, U_m, U_c, $\bar{Q}_m$, $\bar{Q}_c$, $\bar{U}_m$, $\bar{U}_c$, Q, U, and S. Moreover, Q, U, and S can all be expressed in terms of the basic constants Q_c, Q_m, U_c, U_m, S_w, and S_v. We can, therefore, in fact express the values at any time of K, M, C, Y, P, W, V, and G in terms of the constants S_v, S_w, Q_c, Q_m, U_c, U_m, $\bar{Q}_c$, $\bar{Q}_m$, $\bar{U}_c$, $\bar{U}_m$, r_c, r_m, R_m, R_c, and l, and of the three initial factor supplies K_0, L_0, and N_0.

But let us return to the case of steady growth. Let us suppose that at time o the point had already been reached in the development of the economy described by equations (3.26) to (3.35) at which k_0 was equal to $\dfrac{r_m + \bar{Q}_m l}{1 - \bar{U}_m}$ and, therefore,

$$\frac{Y_0}{K_0 P_0} = \frac{r_m + \bar{Q}_m l}{S(1 - \bar{U}_m)}$$

(see (3.24)). The economy starts from the stage at which the rate of capital accumulation, k, and the ratio of income to the value of capital stock $\left(\dfrac{Y}{KP}\right)$ both remain unchanged. Let us further simplify our model by assuming, as in Section (2) above, that there are only two factors (L and K), that there are constant returns to scale, and that factors are paid rewards equal to the value of their marginal products, so that

$$Q_m = \bar{Q}_m = 1 - U_m = 1 - \bar{U}_m \text{ and } Q_c = \bar{Q}_c = 1 - U_c = 1 - \bar{U}_c.$$

Then by simplification of equations (3.26) to (3.35) we have:

$$K = K_0 \exp\left\{\left(\frac{r_m}{Q_m} + l\right)t\right\}$$

$$M = \frac{Y_0}{P_0} S \exp\left\{\left(\frac{r_m}{Q_m} + l\right)t\right\}$$

$$C = Y_0(1 - S)\ \exp\left\{\left(\frac{r_c Q_m + r_m(1 - Q_c)}{Q_m} + l\right)t\right\}$$

$$Y = Y_0 \exp\left\{\left(\frac{r_c Q_m + r_m(1 - Q_c)}{Q_m} + l\right)t\right\}$$

$$P = P_0 \exp\left(\frac{r_c Q_m - r_m Q_c}{Q_m}t\right)$$

$$W = \frac{Y_0}{L_0} Q \exp\left(\frac{r_c Q_m + r_m(1 - Q_c)}{Q_m}t\right)$$

$$V = \frac{Y_0}{K_0 P_0}(1 - Q)$$

From this it can be seen that K and M will both grow at a rate equal to $\dfrac{r_m}{Q_m} + l$, C and Y at a rate equal to $r_c + r_m \dfrac{1 - Q_c}{Q_m} + l$, W at a rate equal to $r_c + r_m \dfrac{1 - Q_c}{Q_m}$, while V (the rate of profit) will remain constant. We can verify from the above equations for K, Y, and P that $\dfrac{Y}{KP}$, the ratio of income to the value of stock of capital, will also remain constant. We can also see that $\dfrac{W}{PV}$ (the ratio of the cost of using a worker to that of using a machine) will rise at a rate equal to $\dfrac{r_m}{Q_m}$. P will grow at a rate equal to $r_c - r_m \dfrac{Q_c}{Q_m}$; in other words P will go up (or down) according as $\dfrac{r_c}{r_m} \gtrless \dfrac{Q_c}{Q_m}$. A high level of r_c relatively to r_m will cause the costs of machines to fall less quickly than the cost of consumption goods; and a low level of Q_c relatively to Q_m will mean that the rise in the cost of using a worker relatively to the cost of using a machine will raise the cost of producing labour-intensive capital goods rather than the cost of producing machinery-intensive consumption goods.

Finally, if we suppose that both industries displayed the same conditions of production (i.e. $r_c = r_m = r$ and $Q_c = Q_m = Q$), i.e. in fact that there was only one industry we could reduce the above equations to:

$$K = K_0 \exp\left[\left(\frac{r}{Q} + l\right)t\right]$$

$$M = \frac{Y_0}{P_0} S \exp\left[\left(\frac{r}{Q} + l\right)t\right]$$

$$C = Y_0(1 - S) \exp\left[\left(\frac{r}{Q} + l\right)t\right]$$

$$Y = Y_0 \exp\left[\left(\frac{r}{Q} + l\right)t\right]$$

$$P = P_0 = \text{constant}$$

$$W = \frac{Y_0}{L_0} Q \exp\left(\frac{r}{Q} t\right)$$

$$V = \frac{Y}{K_0 P_0}(1 - Q) = \text{constant}.$$

$\dfrac{K}{L}, \dfrac{M}{L}, \dfrac{C}{L}, \dfrac{Y}{L}$, and W would all grow at the rate $\dfrac{r}{Q}$, and P and V would remain constant. This perhaps reduces the Neo-Classical Model of Steady Equilibrium Growth to its ultimate and most basic form.

Depreciation by Sudden Death

Consider a machine which is produced and installed in year 0, which lasts for T years, and produces the same annual gross profit A in each of the T years of its life, namely in each of the years 1 to T inclusive. If I is the (constant) rate of interest the present value (i.e. value in year 0) of the gross profit which it will produce in year 1 is $\dfrac{A}{1+I}$; the value in year 0 of the profit which it will produce in year 2 is $\dfrac{A}{(1+I)^2}$, and so on. The present value of the machine is the present value of all the T annual profits which it will produce in years 1 to T and this is equal to

$$\frac{A}{B}+\frac{A}{B^2}+ \ldots +\frac{A}{B^{T-1}}+\frac{A}{B^T}$$

where $B = 1+I$. The sum of the above geometric series is $\dfrac{A}{I}\left(1-\dfrac{1}{B^T}\right)$ and this represents the value of the machine in year 0. In year 1 the machine will have only $T-1$ instead of T years of profit-earning ahead of it and by a similar process of reasoning its value in year 1 will be equal to $\dfrac{A}{I}\left(1-\dfrac{1}{B^{T-1}}\right)$; and so on for its value in years 2, 3, 4, etc. This series of diminishing values of the machine as it grows older is shown in row (a) of Table II on page 182. Its value diminishes from $\dfrac{A}{I}\left(1-\dfrac{1}{B^T}\right)$ in the year in which it is installed and becomes zero in year T, the year in which the machine yields its last profit and collapses.

It is necessary for the owner of the machine to accumulate from annual depreciation allowances over the T years of the machine's life a sum which by the Tth year will equal $\dfrac{A}{I}\left(1-\dfrac{1}{B^T}\right)$, which will equal the cost of buying a new machine if (as we are assuming) the cost of a machine is equal to the market value of a new machine. As explained in the text there are many principles on which this can be done. Here we shall start by examining what in the text has been called the 'fixed-annuity' method of depreciation; for we shall claim in this Appendix that for a machine with a fixed length of life and with equal earning power in each year of life, operating in an economy with a constant rate of interest, the 'fixed-annuity' method of depreciation is the rational one. For it can be shown that in these conditions it is this method of depreciation which both maintains the value of the owner's total capital constant over the life of the machine and maintains the owner's net income from his capital constant over the life of the machine.

This can be shown from Table II on page 182 in the following way. Consider the depreciation allowance which is necessary to maintain the value of the owner's capital each year. From row (a) of Table II it can be seen that the value of the machine in year 0 is $\frac{A}{I}\left(1 - \frac{1}{B^T}\right)$ and in year 1 it is only $\frac{A}{I}\left(1 - \frac{1}{B^{T-1}}\right)$; it has

fallen by the difference between these two expressions or by $\frac{A}{B^T}$. Out of his current receipts in year 1 the owner must, therefore, put $\frac{A}{B^T}$ to his depreciation fund to make up for the loss of value

of his machine between year 0 and 1. This figure of $\frac{A}{B^T}$ is, therefore, shown under year 1 in row (b) of Table II. Similarly in year 2 he must add $\frac{A}{B^{T-1}}$ to his depreciation fund in order to off-

set the fall in the value of his machine between years 1 and 2. And so on for the rest of the series in row (b) of Table II.

Now it can be shown that the 'depreciation allowance' of row (b) which rises from $\frac{A}{B^T}$ in year 1 to $\frac{A}{B}$ in year T (the last year of

the machine's life) is equivalent to a constant 'transfer to the depreciation fund' of $\frac{A}{B^T}$ each year. This can be seen by examin-

ing the figures in row (c) of the table, which show under each year the total amount which will have been accumulated in the depreciation fund up to that year. Thus up to year $N-1$ the total depreciation allowances which will have been put into the depreciation fund will be the sum of the figures in row (b) from year 1 to year $N-1$ inclusive or

$$\frac{A}{B^T} + \frac{A}{B^{T-1}} + \cdots + \frac{A}{B^{T-N}}$$

which is equal to $\frac{A}{IB^T}(B^{N-1} - 1)$. But in the next year, year N, interest on securities in the depreciation fund will be received equal to I times this amount or to $\frac{A}{B^T}(B^{N-1} - 1)$. As can be seen from row (b) a depreciation allowance of $\frac{A}{B^{T-N+1}}$ will be made in year N, but $\frac{A}{B^T}(B^{N-1} - 1)$ of this can be met out of interest paid on the capital previously accumulated in the depreciation fund, which leaves

$$\frac{A}{B^{T-N+1}} - \frac{A}{B^T}(B^N - 1)$$

or $\frac{A}{B^T}$ to be met from a 'transfer from profits to the depreciation fund'. In other words, the series in row (b) of Table II represents a constant 'transfer from profits to the depreciation fund' of $\frac{A}{B^T}$ with the addition of the growing sum of interest on the accumulated depreciation fund.

It can also be shown that this principle of depreciation leaves the owner's net disposable income from all sources constant over time. Consider his position in year N. (i) He has, as in every year of the machine's life, a gross profit of A. (ii) He has the interest on the depreciation fund accumulated up to the year $N-1$ or

$$I \times \frac{A}{IB^T}(B^{N-1} - 1).$$

(iii) But he has to put aside a depreciation allowance of $\frac{A}{B^{T-N+1}}$

to maintain the value of his capital intact. His net disposable income in year N is, therefore,

$$A + \frac{A}{B^T}(B^{N-1} - 1) - \frac{A}{B^{T-N+1}} = A\left(1 - \frac{1}{B^T}\right).$$

But this net income is independent of the value given to N and remains constant, therefore, throughout the T years of the machine's life.

Let us next consider a firm which possesses not one machine which it replaces every T years, but a 'balanced' set of machines, (one new one, one one-year old, one two-years old, and so on) of which one comes to the end of its life and needs to be replaced each year. Then the total value of its 'balanced' set of T machines will be the sum of the values in row (a) of Table II for a single machine as it passes through the T years of its life; for it will possess one machine in each age group. Now the sum of the figures in row (a) of Table II is, as shown in the right-hand column of the row,

$$\frac{TA}{I}\left\{1 - \frac{1}{IT}\left(1 - \frac{1}{B^T}\right)\right\}.$$

On the other hand a new machine has the value $\frac{A}{I}\left(1 - \frac{1}{B^T}\right)$—as shown in the first figure in row (a) of Table II—so that a 'new' set (i.e. a set of T new machines) would be worth $\frac{TA}{I}\left(1 - \frac{1}{B^T}\right)$. The ratio of the value of a 'balanced' set of machines to the value of the same number of new machines is, therefore,

$$\frac{1 - \frac{1}{IT}}{1 - \frac{1}{B^T}}.^1$$

The above relationship is true whatever principle of depreciation is adopted. But if we assume that our firm with the 'balanced' set of machines adopts the rational 'fixed-annuity' principle for

---

[1] This is the formula reached by Champernowne and Kahn (*loc. cit*) if we write it in the form which it would take if there were continuous compounding of interest, namely, $\frac{1}{1 - \exp(-IT)} - \frac{1}{IT}$.

the depreciation of each of its machines we can calculate for a 'balanced' set of machines the depreciation fund, the total capital value of machines and depreciation fund, and the net annual income from the machines and depreciation fund. This is done in the remaining figures in the last column of Table II. As far as the annual depreciation allowance is concerned, this will be equal to the depreciation allowance made in the first year of the life of one machine plus that made in the second year of life of another machine, and so on; it will in fact be equal to the sum of the figures in row (b) for a single machine; and this, as shown in the right-hand column of row (b) is equal to $\frac{A}{I}\left(1 - \frac{1}{B^T}\right)$. This is equal to the cost of a new machine, so that with a 'balanced' set of machines the total depreciation allowance made in respect of all the T machines in any one year will be just sufficient to replace one machine each year[1].

The total depreciation fund outstanding at any one moment of time in respect of the balanced set of T machines will be equal to the sum of the depreciation funds accumulated one in respect of a machine one year old, one in respect of a machine two years old, and so on; and this total depreciation fund will be the sum of the funds in row (c) of Table II for a single machine passing through its various ages from 1 to T years. But at this point a little care is necessary. We are dealing with discreet intervals of a year; on some day in each year (say, 30th June) a machine collapses and immediately afterwards (say, 1st July) a part of the depreciation fund is used up to purchase a new machine. Now in summing the value of the 'balanced' set of machines in row (a) we assumed that we had one brand-new machine worth $\frac{A}{I}\left(1 - \frac{1}{B^T}\right)$.

In other words, we reckoned the value of the machines in existence not on 30th June but on 1st July. But whereas on 30th June we

---

[1] In Table II this is calculated for the rational 'fixed-annuity' method of depreciation. But it is in fact true of any depreciation method provided that it observes only the elementary principle that the sum of the depreciation allowances over the T years of life of a machine will be sufficient to meet the cost of a new machine in the Tth year. For if this is so, then the sum of the depreciation allowances made in any one year in respect of T machines, each in one of the T years of life of a machine, will also obviously sum up to the cost of one new machine.

possessed in the depreciation fund the amount of the depreciation fund accumulated in respect of the machine just on the point of collapse—namely, the $\dfrac{A}{I}\left(1-\dfrac{1}{B^T}\right)$ shown in row (c) as the depreciation fund accumulated in respect of a machine in its Tth and final year of profit-earning—on 1st July we possess a new machine instead of this part of the total depreciation fund. In other words, when we come to assess the total value of the capital of our firm we must not count both the value of a brand-new machine—i.e. the $\dfrac{A}{I}\left(1-\dfrac{1}{B^T}\right)$ in the column under year o in row (a)—and also the value of a finally and fully accumulated depreciation fund— i.e. the $\dfrac{A}{I}\left(1-\dfrac{1}{B^T}\right)$ in the column under year T in row (a). If we were reckoning as at 30th June each year we must reckon capital values by summing the figures for the T years from columns 1 to T for both the value of the machines (row (a)) and the value of their depreciation funds (row (c)); but as we are reckoning as at 1st July each year we must reckon capital values by summing the figures for the T years from columns o to $T-1$ for both the value of the machines (row (a)) and for the value of their depreciation funds (row (c)).

If we do this we obtain (in the right-hand column of row (c)) the value of

$$\frac{TA}{I}\left\{\frac{1}{IT}\left(1-\frac{1}{B^T}\right)-\frac{1}{B^T}\right\}$$

for the value of the total accumulated depreciation fund. The sum of this plus the value of all the T machines (given in the right-hand column of row (a)) is $\dfrac{TA}{I}\left(1-\dfrac{1}{B^T}\right)$ and this is shown in the right-hand column of row (e). This figure, it is to be observed, is T times the (constant) figure for the total capital value of machine and depreciation fund for the single machine in row (e), the 'balanced' set of T machines being in this case simply T times the (constant) total capital value of one machine plus its depreciation fund. Moreover, it is also to be observed that this total capital value for the 'balanced' set of T machines plus the corresponding total depreciation fund *which will be accumulated on the rational principle of the 'fixed-annuity' for each machine* is equal to T times the value of a new machine. In other words, with (i) a 'balanced' set of machines and (ii) the rational 'fixed-annuity' principle for depreciating each machine, the total value of the firm's capital will be equal to the value of T brand-new machines, but of this a proportion $\left(\dfrac{1}{1-\dfrac{1}{B^T}}-\dfrac{1}{IT}\right)$ will represent the value of the machines at any one time and the remainder will represent the securities held in the depreciation fund.

The net disposable income available for the owners of the firm is shown in the right-hand column of row (d) of Table II. This can in fact be reckoned in any of three different ways. First, it is equal to the sum of the (constant) net incomes received in respect of each of the T machines of different ages shown in the columns 1 to T for a single machine. Second, it is equal to the total capital value of the firm—i.e. the $\dfrac{TA}{I}\left(1-\dfrac{1}{B^T}\right)$ in the right-hand column of row (e)—multiplied by the rate of interest, I; for the net disposable income is the current yield on the constant capital value of the firm. Third, it is equal to the sum of TA (i.e. the gross profit of A earned on each of T machines) *plus*

$$TA\left\{\frac{1}{IT}\left(1-\frac{1}{B^T}\right)-\frac{1}{B^T}\right\}$$

(i.e. the securities held in the depreciation fund as shown in column (c) multiplied by the rate of interest earned on them) *minus* $\dfrac{A}{I}\left(1-\dfrac{1}{B^T}\right)$ (i.e. the total depreciation allowance which must be set aside each year).

Consider next a firm which is growing steadily in the sense that the number of machines which it purchases each year grows, and has for long been growing, at the steady proportionate rate of h. That is to say, if $h = 5$ per cent per annum, then every year the total number of machines installed in the firm (to meet replacement and capital expansion) is 5 per cent greater than the number installed in the previous year. Let $1 + h = X$. Suppose that the number of machines installed T years ago was H; then the replacement expenditure this year will be equal to H times the cost of a new machine, or $\dfrac{HA}{I}\left(\mathrm{I}-\dfrac{\mathrm{I}}{B^T}\right)$, since all these H machines will need replacement this year.

But what will be the size of the total depreciation allowances made this year in respect of the whole of the firm's present set of machines? We will reckon this sum on the two assumptions of the 'fixed-annuity' principle for depreciation and the 'straight-line' principle. This is shown in Table III on page 183. We consider (row (a)) the last T years. T years ago H machines were installed, $T-\mathrm{I}$ years ago HX machines were installed, $T-2$ years ago HX^2 machines were installed and so on up to the last year when HX^{T-1} machines were installed (row (b)). We then consider (in rows (c) and (d)) the depreciation allowances which will have to be made in year o in respect of each of these existing batches of machines of different age groups.

Consider first depreciation on the 'fixed-annuity' principle. This year there are H machines installed T years ago and now about to collapse; on each of these (as we see from the column T of row (b) of Table II) a depreciation allowance of $\dfrac{A}{B}$ must be made, so that in the present year o we must make a depreciation allowance of $\dfrac{HA}{B}$ in respect of machines installed T years ago. Similarly, this year there are HX machines installed $T-\mathrm{I}$ years ago (row (b) column $-[T-\mathrm{I}]$ of Table III) and on each of these machines which are $T-\mathrm{I}$ years old a depreciation allowance of $\dfrac{A}{B^2}$ must be made (row (b) column $T-\mathrm{I}$ of Table II) so that in respect of this batch of machines we must this year make a total depreciation allowance of $HX\dfrac{A}{B^2}$ (row (c) column $-[T-\mathrm{I}]$ of Table III). And so on for the rest of the series in row (c) of Table III. The total depreciation allowance which must be made this year in respect of all machines (new and old) in existence this year is the sum of all the figures in row (c) of Table III or

$$HA\dfrac{\mathrm{I}-\left(\dfrac{X}{B}\right)^T}{I-h}.$$

We can make the same type of calculation for the case of 'straight-line' depreciation. A new machine is worth $\frac{A}{B}\left(1 - \frac{1}{B^T}\right)$ as shown in row (a), column o, of Table II. The 'straight-line' method of depreciation means that this cost must be divided into T equal parts and this same constant amount of $\frac{A}{IT}\left(1 - \frac{1}{B^T}\right)$ must be charged against each machine in every year of its life. Now our expanding firm will have $H\frac{X^T - 1}{h}$ machines in its stock in year o, as is shown in the right-hand column of row (b) of Table III for the sum of all the machines installed over the last T years. Therefore, the total depreciation allowance which must be made this year in respect of all existing machines will be

$$\frac{A}{IT}\left(1 - \frac{1}{B^T}\right)H\frac{X^T - 1}{h}$$

as shown in the right-hand column of row (d) of Table III.

We have already shown that replacement expenditure in this year o will be $\frac{HA}{I}\left(1 - \frac{1}{B^T}\right)$. It follows that the ratio of depreciation allowances to replacement expenditure this year will be equal to

$$\frac{I}{I-h} \cdot \frac{B^T - X^T}{B^T - 1}$$

in the case of the 'fixed-annuity' method of depreciation and to

$$\frac{X^T - 1}{hT}$$

in the case of the 'straight-line' method of depreciation[1].

---

[1] This last formula is equal to $\frac{\exp(hT) - 1}{hT}$ if we write it in the form appropriate to continuous compounding of growth. It is found in this form in E. D. Domar's 'Depreciation, Replacement, and Growth' (reprinted in his *Essays in the Theory of Economic Growth*).

Table II.—Value of Machines and Depreciation Funds

Year	Single Machines: Installed in year 0 and yielding a gross profit of A in each of the T succeeding years, 1 to T.								'Balanced' Set of Machines (i.e., Set of T machines, one from each group of the T age-groups).
	0	1	2 ...	$N{-}1$	N	$T{-}1$	T	
Value of Machinery (a)	$\frac{A}{I}\left(I-\frac{I}{B^T}\right)$	$\frac{A}{I}\left(I-\frac{I}{B^{T-1}}\right)$	$\frac{A}{I}\left(I-\frac{I}{B^{T-2}}\right)$ ...	$\frac{A}{I}\left(I-\frac{I}{B^{T-N+1}}\right)$	$\frac{A}{I}\left(I-\frac{I}{B^{T-N}}\right)$ ...	$\frac{A}{I}\left(I-\frac{I}{B}\right)$	0	$\sum_0^{T-1}=\frac{TA}{I}\left\{I-\frac{I}{IT}\left(I-\frac{I}{B^T}\right)\right\}$
Depreciation Allowance on 'Fixed Annuity' Principle (b)	0	$\frac{A}{B^T}$	$\frac{A}{B^{T-1}}$ ...	$\frac{A}{B^{T-N+2}}$	$\frac{A}{B^{T-N+1}}$ ...	$\frac{A}{B^2}$	$\frac{A}{B}$	$\sum_1^{T}=\frac{A}{I}\left(I-\frac{I}{B^T}\right)$
Accumulated Depreciation Fund. (c)	0	$\frac{A}{B^T}$	$\frac{A}{IB^T}(B^2-I)$ ...	$\frac{A}{IB^T}(B^{N-1}-I)$	$\frac{A}{IB^T}(B^N-I)$ ...	$\frac{A}{IB^T}(B^{T-1}-I)$	$\frac{A}{I}\left(I-\frac{I}{B^T}\right)$	$\sum_0^{T-1}=\frac{TA}{I}\left\{\frac{I}{IT}\left(I-\frac{I}{B^T}\right)-\frac{I}{B^T}\right\}$
Net Income[1] (d)	0	$A\left(I-\frac{I}{B^T}\right)$	$A\left(I-\frac{I}{B^T}\right)$ ...	$A\left(I-\frac{I}{B^T}\right)$	$A\left(I-\frac{I}{B^T}\right)$ ...	$A\left(I-\frac{I}{B^T}\right)$	$A\left(I-\frac{I}{B^T}\right)$	$\sum_1^{T}=TA\left(I-\frac{I}{B^T}\right)$
Total Capital Value[2] (e)	$\frac{A}{I}\left(I-\frac{I}{B^T}\right)$	$\frac{A}{I}\left(I-\frac{I}{B^T}\right)$	$\frac{A}{I}\left(I-\frac{I}{B^T}\right)$ ...	$\frac{A}{I}\left(I-\frac{I}{B^T}\right)$	$\frac{A}{I}\left(I-\frac{I}{B^T}\right)$ ...	$\frac{A}{I}\left(I-\frac{I}{B^T}\right)$	$\frac{A}{I}\left(I-\frac{I}{B^T}\right)$	$\sum_0^{T-1}=\frac{TA}{I}\left(I-\frac{I}{B^T}\right)$

[1] Gross Profit plus Interest on Depreciation Fund of Previous Year minus Depreciation Allowance of Current Year.

[2] Value of Machinery plus Accumulated Depreciation Fund.

Table III.—Total Depreciation Allowance on Growing Capital Stock

Year in which machines installed. (a)	$-T$	$-(T-1)$	....	-2	-1	
Number of machines installed. (b)	H	HX	....	HX^{T-2}	HX^{T-1}	$\Sigma = H\dfrac{X^T-1}{h}$
Depreciation Allowance made in year 0 in respect of these machines: (i) 'Fixed-Annuity' Method of Depreciation. (c)	$H\dfrac{A}{B}$	$HX\dfrac{A}{B^2}$	....	$HX^{T-2}\dfrac{A}{B^{T-1}}$	$HX^{T-1}\dfrac{A}{B^T}$	$\Sigma = HA\dfrac{\left(\dfrac{X}{B}\right)^T-1}{h-1}$
(ii) 'Straight-Line' Method of Depreciation. (d)	$H\dfrac{A}{IT}\left(1-\dfrac{1}{B^T}\right)$	$HX\dfrac{A}{IT}\left(1-\dfrac{1}{B^T}\right)$	....	$HX^{T-2}\dfrac{A}{IT}\left(1-\dfrac{1}{B^T}\right)$	$HX^{T-1}\dfrac{A}{IT}\left(1-\dfrac{1}{B^T}\right)$	$\Sigma = H\dfrac{X^T-1}{h}\cdot\dfrac{A}{IT}\left(1-\dfrac{1}{B^T}\right)$

Summary of Notation Used

A (in Appendix III) = annual gross profit on a machine.

B (in Appendix III) = $1+I$ = one plus the rate of interest.

C = output of consumption goods.

G = rent per unit of land.

H (in Appendix III) = number of machines installed T years ago.

I (in Appendix III) = rate of interest.

K_c = stock of machines used to produce consumption goods.

K_m = stock of machines used to produce capital goods.

K = K_c+K_m = total stock of machines.

L_c = labour employed in producing consumption goods.

L_m = labour employed in producing capital goods.

L = L_c+L_m = total labour employed.

M = output of capital goods.

N_c = land used to produce consumption goods.

N_m = land used to produce capital goods.

N = N_c+N_m = total land in use.

P = price of capital goods.

Q_c = the proportion of the value of the output of consumption goods which would go to wages if the wage rate equalled the marginal product of labour.[1]

Q_m = the proportion of the value of the output of capital goods which would go to wages if the wage rate equalled the marginal product of labour.[1]

Q = the proportion of the national income which would go to wages if the wage rate equalled the marginal product of labour.[1]

r = rate of technical progress.

r_l, r_k, r_n = the growth rates of the marginal products of L, K, and N respectively due to technical progress.

r_c, r_m = the rate of technical progress in the industries producing C and M respectively.

r_{lc} = the growth rate in the marginal product of L in the industry producing C due to technical progress, and similarly for r_{lm}, $r_{kc}, r_{km}, r_{nc},$ and r_{nm}.

R_c = a constant in the production function of consumption goods.

R_m = a constant in the production function of capital goods.

S_v = the proportion of profits saved.

S_w = the proportion of wages saved.

S_g = the proportion of rents saved.

---

[1] In Section 3 of Appendix II $Q_c, Q_m,$ and Q are the actual proportions which go to wages, while $\hat{Q}_c, \hat{Q}_m,$ and $\hat{Q}$ are the proportions which would go to wages if the wage rate were equal to the marginal product of labour.

S = the proportion of the national income saved.

t = time.

T (in Appendix III) = length of life of a machine.

U_c = the proportion of the value of the output of consumption goods which would go to profits if profit per machine was equal to the marginal product of a machine.[1]

U_m = the proportion of the value of the output of capital goods which would go to profits if profit per machine was equal to the marginal product of a machine.[1]

U = the proportion of the national income which would go to profits if profit per machine was equal to the marginal product of a machine.[1]

V = rate of profit.

W = wage rate.

X (in Appendix III) = $1+h$ = one plus the growth rate in the number of machines installed.

Y = net national income.

Z = the proportion of the national income which would go to rent if rent per unit of land were equal to the marginal product of land.

$\beta_l = r_l - r$ and similarly for β_k and β_n.

$\beta_{lc} = r_{lc} - r_c$ and similarly for β_{ln}, β_{kc}, β_{km}, β_{nc}, and β_{nm}.

$\beta_c = \beta_{lc} - \beta_{kc} = r_{lc} - r_{kc}$ and similarly for β_m.

$\beta = \beta_l - \beta_k = r_l - r_k$.

$\epsilon_k = -\dfrac{V}{K}\dfrac{\partial K}{\partial V}$

$\gamma = S_v - S_w$.

$\lambda = Q_c - Q_m$.

$\mu = w - p - v$ = the growth rate in the ratio of wage per man to profit per machine.

σ_{kl}, σ_{nl}, and σ_{kn} = elasticities of substitution between K and L, between N and L, and between K and N respectively.

σ_c and σ_m = elasticities of substitution between men and machines in the consumption-good industry and in the capital-good industry respectively.

$\bar{\sigma}$ = weighted average of σ_c and σ_m.

$\overline{\sigma\beta}$ = weighted average of $\sigma_c\beta_c$ and $\sigma_m\beta_m$.

Note that in all cases except t a small letter represents the growth rate in the corresponding capital letter. Thus

$$y = \frac{1}{Y}\frac{dY}{dt}, \quad k = \frac{1}{K}\frac{dK}{dt}, \text{ etc.}$$

---

[1] In Section 3 of Appendix II U_c, U_m, and U are the actual proportions going to profits and $\overline{U}_c$, $\overline{U}_m$, and $\overline{U}$ are the proportions which would go to profits if profit per machine was equal to the marginal product of a machine.

GEORGE ALLEN & UNWIN LTD
London: 40 Museum Street, W.C.1

Auckland: 24 Wyndham Street
Bombay: 15 Graham Road, Ballard Estate, Bombay 1
Cape Town: 109 Long Street
Buenos Aires: Escritorio 454-459, Florida 165
Calcutta: 17 Chittaranjan Avenue, Calcutta 13
Hong Kong: F1/12 Mirador Mansions, Kowloon
Karachi: Karachi Chambers, McLeod Road
Mexico: Villalongin 32-10, Piso, Mexico 5, D.F.
New Delhi: 13-14 Ajmeri Gate Extension, New Delhi 1
Sao Paulo: Avenida 9 de Julho 1138-Ap. 51
Singapore: 36c Princep Street, Singapore 7
Sydney: N.S.E.: Bradbury House, 55 York Street
Toronto: 91 Wellington Street West

BY J. E. MEADE

PLANNING AND THE PRICE MECHANISM

To plan or not to plan? This book outlines a solution to our present economic problems which makes the fullest use of the price mechanism and of free initiative and competition, but which involves the socialisation of certain monopolistic concerns and the State control of the price mechanism in such a way as to maintain full employment, to achieve an equitable distribution of income and property and to restore equilibrium to our international balance of payments. It is an outline of that 'middle way' which the author calls the Liberal-Socialist solution.

'Altogether this is a valuable little book which should make not only the rationale of enlightened Socialism and the mechanics of planning but the nature of Britain's present economic dilemma a good deal clearer to its readers.' —*Spectator*.

Cr. 8vo. 10s. 6d. net

GEOMETRY OF INTERNATIONAL TRADE

In the course of writing his treatise on the 'Theory of International Economic Policy,' the author elaborated a geometrical technique to aid his own analysis of a number of the problems which he encountered. 'A Geometry of International Trade' is a systematic exposition of this geometric method. It contains some fifty geometrical diagrams with about 100 pages of descriptive text. It puts together into a single coherent account the modern geometrical analysis of the theory of international trade which at present can be studied only by consulting a large number of separate articles. In addition, Professor Meade makes a number of original contributions, notably in the geometrical treatment of domestic production, of the balance of payments, and of import and export duties. It is probable that this work also will become a landmark in the development of its subject.

Demy 8vo. 28s. net

PROBLEMS OF ECONOMIC UNION

In his new book, Professor Meade discusses the main problems in the formation of an Economic Union of one sort or another between a number of independent states. In particular he analyses the extent to which national governments would have to give up their freedom of action in domestic monetary, budgetary, fiscal, and economic policies if they were to form an effective economic union. He covers the problems of commercial policy, of financial and exchange-rate policies, of migration and investment policies, and of the finance of a common defence budget.

Professor Meade's sustained lucidity will appeal to a wide audience of laymen as well as to specialists, while his peculiar qualifications for writing on this subject need no emphasis.

Demy 8vo. 9s. 6d. net

BRITISH ECONOMY 1920-1957

A. J. YOUNGSON

The greater part of this book consists of an attempt to describe and account for the course of British economic development since the end of the post-war boom in 1920, a subject which has hardly been tackled at any length or in any convenient form. The coverage is general, but the author pays particular attention to changes in the industrial structure, to international trade, financial policy and fluctuations in the level of activity. The final section is devoted to a fascinating discussion of government economic policy throughout the period, in which the author seeks to trace the relation between policy and the ideas put forward at the time by economists such as Pigou, Robertson and Keynes.

The basic intention is to provide a book which deals with the economic history of Britain since 1920 as fully and as consistently as many books now deal with the nineteenth century. Primarily suitable for undergraduates, the book will also make a strong appeal to the wider public interested in the trends of recent economic development. The author's discussion of economic policy will also interest those who already have some knowledge of the academic writings of the period. The picture which emerges of economic development and policy as a whole in the past thirty seven years will greatly contribute to our general understanding of current problems.

Demy 8vo. 28s. net

FISCAL POLICY IN UNDERDEVELOPED COUNTRIES

RAJA J. CHELLIAH

The central thesis of this important book is an application of recent advances in the theory of fiscal policy to the promotion of economic development, while at the same time diminishing inequalities. The author demonstrates, without resorting to esoteric arguments obscure to the general reader, why advanced and underdeveloped countries need different policies, and thereby makes a distinct contribution to fiscal theory.

The book will be of interest to those concerned with the theory of public finance, to those responsible for practical policy, and particularly to economists working in underdeveloped areas. What makes it very topical is the growing awareness of economic problems in general, and in particular the desire, noticeable of late in all these countries, to employ taxation in the service of economic development. India is a notable case, which Dr. Chelliah handles on the basis of his own study, research and personal experience. He analyses and evaluates the recommendations of the Indian Taxation Enquiry Commission (1953-54) and those in Mr. Kaldor's recent report to the Indian Government.

Demy 8vo. 20s. net

AN EXPENDITURE TAX

NICHOLAS KALDOR

This book examines the idea that the taxation of individuals should be based not on their income, but on their expenditure. The idea in itself, as the author states in the Introduction, is not new: it has attracted a succession of eminent political economists from John Stuart Mill's day to our own—and indeed the common sense case for taxing people on what they consume rather than on what they earn—on what they take out of the pool rather than what they put in —was succinctly put 300 years ago by Thomas Hobbes.

In this book the author challenges the traditional view that an expenditure tax must be looked upon either as an administrative impossibility (the last two chapters are devoted to the detailed practical workings of a progressive expenditure tax system), or as a simple sales tax which would necessarily be highly regressive in its incidence. He suggests that a beginning could be made by replacing our present surtax scheme by an expenditure tax; and, drawing attention to the revolutionary implications of such a step, particularly at this time when the rich 'not only live beyond their taxed income, but to an appreciable extent forgo having such income', argues that it would be necessary to apply a schedule of rates far more moderate than the present surtax schedule if the fabric of society were to be preserved reasonably intact.

'Mr. Kaldor's closely reasoned, but highly readable and stimulating, arguments ought to be seriously considered—and not least by Mr. Butler if he is, as he says, open to new ideas.' *The Observer.*

Demy 8vo. 20s. net

CAN INFLATION BE CONTROLLED ?

HAROLD G. MOULTON

Can inflation be controlled in war or peace ? By Government ? By Capital, by Labour or both ? Should it be controlled at all ? Is there any hope ahead for stable prices ?

In this detailed study of the causes of price inflation, and from a lifetime of study and experience, Dr. Moulton offers answers to these and other questions. In the process he litters the economic beaches with the wreckage of outmoded and fallacious monetary theories.

Serious students of economics will find here a thorough appraisal of traditional monetary and fiscal policies in the light of the ever-changing economic structure.

La. Cr. 8vo. 21s. net

THE DEVELOPMENT OF THE INDIAN ECONOMY

W. B. REDDAWAY

The attempts which are being made to develop the Indian economy and to enable the Indian people to escape from their traditional poverty; the wisdom of the methods adopted, the prospects of success and the factors limiting the pace of the advance; the assistance which developed countries can render: these are questions about which many people in western countries feel that they are sadly ill-informed.

The author of this book visited India for a year under the auspices of the Center for International Studies, in the hope of learning about such matters on the spot. He had the great advantage of continuous collaboration with senior members of the Planning Commission and with several Organizations engaged in economic research, notably the Indian Statistical Institute. The result is something new in the way of realistic analysis, which lays particular stress on the relationships between different branches of the economy and the different, factors which affect them.

Part I analyses the fundamental nature of the Indian economy, the factors which limit the pace of its development, the influence of population growth, and the crucial importance of international trade (despite its quantitatively small size). The vital importance of expanding agriculture as well as industry and the crucial role of the time factor, emerge clearly from the analysis.

The second part of the book gives a statistical picture of how the Indian economy will develop during the Third Five-Year Plan (1961-1966), if this is successfully executed. It throws new light on the development process by showing the inter-relationship of different parts of the economy in a way that has never previously been attempted, and gives a much more complete picture of what happens to consumers.

Mr. Reddaway gave a preliminary paper on this subject to the British Association for the Advancement of Science in which he aimed—'to make the subject of interest to the professional economist, but also to make it intelligible and stimulating to the non-professional members of the audience'. In his book he is remarkably successful in achieving the same objective.

Sm. Royal 8vo. **30s.** *net*

THE STATE AND THE FARMER

PETER SELF, HERBERT STORING

This book gives the first full account of British agricultural policy and politics since 1945. It deals with the attempts of the Government, working in close co-operation with agricultural organizations, to place British agriculture on a stable and efficient basis. It describes in detail the character and activities of the organizations which protect the interests of farmers, farm workers, and country landowners. It deals particularly with the close 'partnership' which has grown up between the state and the farmers, and with the many vicissitudes and problems which this partnership has encountered.

After a survey of post-war conditions, the authors describe the growth and organization of the National Farmers' Union, the annual price-fixing encounters between Government and Union, and the turbulent controversies which have surrounded agricultural marketing. They then review the experiment in the use of 'sanctions' against incompetent farmers and the work of the local agricultural committees. They next deal with the activities and the special problems of the organized farm-workers and of country landowners. After examining the political strength and limitations of the agricultural interests, and the influence of the 'farmers vote', they attempt a final assessment of post-war agricultural policy and of the partnership between Goverment and farmers.

This book will be of great interest to all who are concerned with the welfare and prosperity of British agriculture, and with the problems which have once again arisen over the methods and aims of state support. It will thus appeal to agricultural economists, to the Agricultural Advisory Service and to students of agriculture, as well as to practising farmers. But it also has much to say of interest to students of politics about the forces which shape public policy, and about the actual power and influence of interest or 'pressure' groups in the modern world. Both authors have developed this special interest against a background of administrative and political knowledge. They have produced a unique and authoritative study of an interesting and important subject.

Demy 8vo. 30s. *net*

PRICING AND EQUILIBRIUM

E. SCHNEIDER

Allen and Unwin have already announced an English version by Mr. Kurt Klappholz of Volume Three of Professor Schneider's famous *Introduction to Economics* under the title *Money, Income and Employment*. Volume Two has already appeared in English under the title *Pricing and Equilibrium*, translated by Professor T. W. Hutchison from the first German edition.

His version has been out of print for some years and Mr. Bennathan's new edition is based on the greatly enlarged sixth German edition. This volume analyses the economic planning of households and firms, i.e. their economic dispositions. Using partial equilibrium analysis, it describes the equilibria corresponding to various dispositions and the effects of changes in dispositions, ending with an exposition of the problem of general micro-economic equilibrium in a stationary economy.

The book is already known as a remarkably effective piece of teaching—a particularly successful exposition for students. It will be welcomed in this enlarged and improved version.

Demy 8vo. 384 *pages* 45s. *net*

LONDON: GEORGE ALLEN & UNWIN LTD